GAAN NGAI
A FESTIVAL OF
THE ZELIANGRONG NAGAS
OF NORTH EAST INDIA

GAAN NGAI
A FESTIVAL OF
THE ZELIANGRONG NAGAS
OF NORTH EAST INDIA

(Research and Documentation)

Jenpuiru Kamei, M.Sc., Ph.D.

North Eastern Zone Cultural Centre,
Ministry of Culture, Government of India, Dimapur

AKANSHA PUBLISHING HOUSE

4649-B/21, Ansari Road, Darya Ganj, New Delhi-110 002 (India)

AKANSHA PUBLISHING HOUSE
4649-B/21, Ansari Road,
Darya Ganj, New Delhi-110 002
Phones : 011-23263193, 09435116718
E-mail : ektabooks@yahoo.com
visit us : www.akanshapublishinghouse.com

Published by
North Eastern Zone Cultural Centre, Ministry of Culture,
Government of India, Dimapur

Gaan Ngai A Festival of the Zeliangrong Nagas of North East India

First Published : 2012

Reprint 2026

ISBN 978-81-8370-326-0

[The responsibility for the facts stated, conclusions reached etc., is entirely that of the author. The publisher is not responsible for them, whatsoever.]

PRINTED IN INDIA

Published by Akansha Publishing House, New Delhi - 110002.

Contents

Preface

Gaan Ngai Festival of the Zeliangrong Nagas of North East India (Research and Documentation) is a research project commissioned by the Ministry of Culture, Government of India through the North Eastern Zone Cultural Centre, Dimapur. I thank Shri Som Kamei, IPS, Director of the NEZCC for the sanction of the project. The Gaan festival is performed by Zeliangrong Nagas in the north east Indian states of Assam, Manipur and Nagaland where the community is inhabited. I have the pleasure to submit this research report within a period of six months. This was the work of my research team which consisted of knowledgeable scholars who kindly agreed to be the consultants of the project. They were Ramkui Newme and Pautanzan Newme of Assam; Dr. Wilubo Chawang and Ms. Tasile N. Zeliang of Nagaland and Chaoba Kamson and Lanbilung Gonmei of Manipur. The consultants gave me prepared notes on the cognate groups of the Zeliangrong community namely, Zeme, Liangmai, Rongmei and Puimei. I also engaged three research assistants who helped me in my field work.

I visited the research field sites of the three states in the month of January and February 2012. The Gaan Ngai festival was celebrated simultaneously on the 13th day of Manipuri month of Wakching coinciding with the month of Pous of the Indian Saka era which fell on 7th January 2012. The Governments of Manipur, Assam and Nagaland declared the festival as government holidays. My visits to the field sites are given in Chapter one of the report. I got assistance from respected elders of the community, ranging from political leaders to the religious community leaders and village level elders including priests.

I would like to thank the following scholars and elders in the completion of my report on Gaan Ngai festival. Meijinlung Kamson, former M.P. of Manipur, Ramkui Newme, President of Zeliangrong Heraka Association, North East India, Pautanzan Newme, General Secretary of Zeliangrong Heraka Association, Chamkandai Kamei, a social and religious leader of Cachar valley of Assam, Chaoba Kamson, General Secretary of Tingkao Ragwang Chapriak Phom (TRC) and his respected colleagues namely Lanbilung Gonmei and Leirenjao Meiringmei who were General Secretaries of TRC. I am grateful to Dr. Wilubo Chawang, Hurui Zeliang, Deputy Speaker of Naga Hoho, Dimapur, Ms. Tasile Zeliang of Jakulie-B and Jagdamba Mall of Kohima for giving me help during my research. I am grateful to Kathuna Daimei of Chingmeirong, Imphal, K.D. Pamei of Kakhulong, Imphal, Kuije Disong of Katang, Lungnihai Rongmei of Thanagong, Khoupum, Deralung Zeme of Jalukie, Gaithaochung Golmei, Khunpu of Majorkhul, R. Tampikhon, Mantri of Majorkhul, Abuina Golmei, Khangchupou of Majorkhul, Khangmeidun Kamei, Gaikompu Phaomei, Gaiguplung Gangmei, and other elders of Majorkhul Khangchu who helped me in my field work. After the completion of my field work, I prepared the final report at the Indian Institute of Advanced Study, Shimla as my father was working there. I thank my father Professor Gangmumei Kamei for his guidance and advice. It was he who introduce me to Zeliangrong history, culture and religion since my childhood. I utilized the facilities available at this distinguished institute for the preparation of my report.

I am also grateful to my mother, Smt. G. Lanshailu who accompanied me during my field work. I thank Ramkui Newme of Haflong and Chamkandai Kamei of Silchar who accompanied me during my field works in the villages of Borohaflong, Lodiram, Asalu, Laisong, Hangrum and Silchar. I also thank Lanchonglung Longmei for his all around assistance during the field work. I am also grateful to Shri Brahma, the Chief Conservator of Forest, Govt. of Assam for providing hospitality at Hangrum village. I am also grateful to the village council and elders of Hangrum village of Assam for their help and advice. I am grateful to the subordinate staff of NEZCC, Athang Kom and Jacky Longmei of Imphal for helping me. I thank my brothers, Dr. Ram Kamei and Shyam Kamei for their encouragement.

Jenpuiru Kamei

Shimla
31st March, 2012

1

Exploring the Naga Festivals

The Post-harvest Festivals

Festivals have been an inseparable part of the life of tribal India for centuries. This is a continuing tradition in modern times. The Indian tribal festivals of nearly 600 tribal groups possess a distinctive quality of their own, standing out from other city festivals happening each other day. The tribal mode of celebration, their costumes, their fineries, their dances, their songs, their languages and ceremonies spreading over far off jungles and mountains make the tribal festivals as a unique cultural and aesthetic experience. Beginning from Jammu and Kashmir in the north to Kerala in the south to Gujarat in the west and Nagaland in the east, the tribal festivals exist in every corner of the states of the country. It has been observed by competent scholars that the tribal festivals in India are mostly religious in nature with a cultural expression in form of dance, music and ceremonies. The tribal festivals are also performed according to their lunar agricultural calendar; festivals have been described for example as seed sowing, weeding, pre-harvest and post-harvest festivals.

The agrarian communities, both peasants and tribals perform with emotional gusto, the post-harvest festivals. In India there are a large number of post-harvest festivals performed by the peasants and tribals. We have great harvest festivals of Pongal performed by Tamils and Malayalis in south India. Pongal defines south India's cultural vivacity. Makar Sankranti is a harvest festival celebrated in most of the north Indian states. The main attraction of this celebration is the kite flying. Lohri, the harvest festival of Punjab is celebrated with the traditional Bhangra dance around the fire. People offer sugarcane, rice and sesame seeds. Folk songs are sung as a thanksgiving for good harvest. We have a unique harvest festival performed by the people of Assam known as Bihu. There are 3 forms of Bihu festival, Rongali Bihu in mid-April, Kati or Kangali Bihu in mid-October and Magh or Bhogali Bihu in mid-January. Magh Bihu or Bhogali Bihu is derived from the word 'Bhoga" meaning eating or enjoyment. It is a harvest festival and the biggest of the 3 Bihus. This is a joyous occasion when the granaries are stocked with recently harvested crop. This festival is marked by seven days of non stop fun and frolic.

Among the tribal post-harvest festivals, Navakhana is such one festival of Chhattisgarh. People present the new harvest crop and liquor as offering before the family deity. The Dimasa of Assam perform the the post-harvest festival known as Bishu Dima. In Meghalaya, Wangala is a post-harvest festival celebrated by the Garo tribe. During this festival the people perform propitiation ceremonies in honour of the deity Patigipa Rarongipa in every village. The people follow the religious rites and rituals with much veneration for a consecutive period of four days and nights. The conclusion of the festival is marked by the warrior dance. Ka Pomblang Nongkrem is a harvest festival and considered to be the most eminent festival of the Khasi community of Meghalaya. Several religious rites and rituals are associated with this festival among which offering of goats (also known as Pomblang ceremony) to the administrative head is the most important. The first day of the festival is marked by a royal dance performance which takes place at the dawn.

Besides the traditional dances sword dance, music, colourful costumes and stunning jewellery enhance the spirit of the festive celebrations.

Chavang Kut is a festival celebrated by the Kuki-Chin-Mizo tribes of Assam, Mizoram and Manipur. Kut literally means a festival. It is the greatest and most joyful festival celebrated every year on 1st November. The Kuts are observed with the arrival of the new crops or after harvesting. The basic philosophy of such festival is that the toiling community must have a short respite and recreation after the year's crop has been reaped. This is an occasion when the people praise God for blessings given to them. Even the poorest forgets his poverty when Kut comes. It is a time for man to rejoice. The rejoicing is universal and every one wishes the occasion to continue. There are four types of Kut festivals as given below:

1. Mim Kut (festival of job's ear)
2. Chang Kut (Paddy festival)
3. Pawl Kut (Harvest festival)
4. Thai lop (festival of vegetables).

Another unique festival performed by the Hmar people is the Sikpui Ruoi (Sikpui festival). The Sikpui Ruoi has no particular date of festival. The Sikpui Ruoi is not celebrated every year. It is celebrated only in the year of abundant harvest, such a year is said to be a year of full granary when the granary is still left with the previous year's yield at the arrival of the new harvest. It is celebrated at a convenient time in December or January. Young men and women take out the previous year's yield and winnow the grain two or three months ahead of Sikpui Ruoi. The term Sikpui Ruoi literally means 'winter feast', Sikpui meaning winter and Ruoi means feast. It is a community festival in which all people participate. It is performed with feast and festival accompanied by songs and dances. It is a remarkable community festival of the Hmars.

Festivals of the Nagas

The Nagas are an agrarian community inhabiting the present state of Nagaland, Assam, Manipur and Arunachal Pradesh in India and the autonomous Naga Region of Burma and they revolve their festivals around agriculture. While celebrating the festivals, the Naga offers prayers to the Supreme God known by different names in their dialects. The festivals are marked with religious sacrifices and celebrated either before sowing season or during the post harvest season. The philosophy behind the festival is that they were celebrated to thank the Almighty for a good harvest. There are various festivals among the Naga tribes, whether pre-harvest, during harvest or post-harvest. We give below the main festivals of various Naga tribes.

Angami

Sekrenyi is celebrated in the month of February and falls on the 25th day of the Angami month of Kezei. It is a 10 days long festival and the Angamis also call it Phousanyi. This festival is associated with a number of rituals and ceremonies. The first ritual is Kizie followed by Dsuseva or touching the sleeping water. The most interesting part of the festival is known as the Thekra Hie where young men and women sing traditional songs throughout the day. Bridge pulling or gate pulling is an important ritual of the festival which falls on the eighth day. People stop working during this time as most of them indulge in feasting and singing.

Ao

Moats Mong is celebrated by the Ao after the sowing is complete. Tsungrem Mong is another festival celebrated on the eve of harvest.

Chakeshang

The Chakeshangs celebrate seven festivals in a year. They are

1. Suhkruhnye – 15th January. It is the most important festival and is spread over 11 days.
2. Ngunye – 1st February
3. Tsakronye – 1st Sunday of March
4. Tsukhanye/Tsukhenyie – 6th May
5. Khuthonye -15th July
6. Turhinye -25th August
7. Thurinye Khiluvat – 1st December

Chang

The Changs observe six festivals in a year. They are Poang Lem, Jeinyu Lem, Kundang Lem, Muong Lem, Naknyu Lem and Monyu Lem. While the first three are monitored by the Haongang Clan, the last three are observed by the Ung Clan.

Khiamniugan

Khiamniugans celebrate Miu which is held in the first week of May every year. It is a festival of forgive and forget. During this festival, the maternal uncle builds a friendly relation with his sister's children.

Konyak

The Konyak celebrates Aoleang Monyu in the first week of April every year. They celebrate the beginning of spring and thank God for the bountiful harvest. It is spread over six days and each day has its own significance. The days are named as Hoi Lai Yah Nyih, Yin Mok Pho Nyih, Yin Mok Shek Nyih, Lingnyu Nyih, Lngha Nyih and Lingshan Nyih.

Lotha

The harvest festival of Lotha is known as Tokhu Emong. It is celebrated for over nine days every year in the first week of November. It is a festival marked with reconciliation, thanks giving and sharing. Past animosity is forgiven and new ties and bonds are formed. The festival is marked with feast, song and dance.

Phom

The Phoms celebrate four festivals in a year. They are Monyu, Moha, Bongvum and Paangmo. Out of these, Monyu is the most important festival and falls in the month of April every year after the sowing season. It is usually celebrated from the 1st of April to the 6th of April. It heralds the New Year and bids farewell to the passing year. While Moha is celebrated to mark the sowing season, Bongvum is the harvest festival.

Pochury

Yemshe is the harvest festival celebrated by the Pochury. People participate in this festival with great pomp and gaiety.

Rengma

Ngada festival is the post harvest festival of the Rengma. It is observed towards the end of November or December for eight days with lots of joy and merry making. The Rengmas hold a strong belief that the spirits of the departed souls of their family members visit their graves and houses during this festival. All eight days of the festival have its own significance and peculiar rituals. People indulge in different rituals and celebrations during the festival.

Sangtam

The Sangtam celebrate about 12 festivals in a year. Amongmong which is celebrated in the first week of

September is the most important festival of the Sangtams. It is celebrated for six days.

Sumi

The Sumi celebrate Ahuna, a post harvest festival with great spirit and fervor. The Sumi people celebrate Tulini, another important festival with drinking and feasting.

Yimchunger

Metumniu festival is the most important festival of the Yimchunger. It is spread over five days and has five different days namely, Shito, Zhihto, Zumto, Khehresuk and Sheresuk.

Other Naga tribes are the Zeliangrong tribes (Zeme, Liangmai and Rongmei) who are spread over three states whom the present project intends to carry out both research and documentation. The Tangkhuls of Manipur have several festivals like Luira phanit which is a seed sowing festival; the greatest post harvest festival of the Tangkhul is the Chumpha festival. This festival is celebrated for seven days in the month of December. The last three days are devoted to social gathering and rejoicing. Unlike other festivals, the women folk play a special role in the festival. The concluding part of the festival ends with a procession within the village.

The Poumai Nagas have several festivals, prominent among which is Laonii festival which is celebrated after rice plantation. It is celebrated in first week of July. In the Lepaona circle of the Poumai Nagas, it is celebrated for nine days; and in the Poumata circle it is celebrated for five days. This festival is a time to enjoy the successful rice plantation to rejuvenate the mind and health of the people. The young men and young women celebrate Laonii in their dormitories (Khekizii, boys' dormitory and Loukizii, girls' dormitory). There are feastings in the dormitories. There are also folk song competitions among the boys and girls. Another festival of the Poumai Nagas is the Thounii. During this festival, traditional dances, songs and indigenous games are performed. Paoki festival is a plantation festival of the Poumai Nagas celebrated for bountiful harvest.

The Maos, Marams, Thangals, Anals and Marings have their own festivals. Our concentration is on the festivals of the Zeliangrong tribe which will be described in the subsequent chapters.

Discovering the Zeliangrong Festivals

I discover the beauty of the Zeliangrong festivals through the methodology which is being adopted in this research programme. It is an anthropological and historical method. The communities selected for our investigation are the Zeliangrong tribe covering the cognate groups of Zeme, Liangmai and Rongmei. To study the festivals of the groups, we applied the anthropological and historical method. We also applied participant observer method in order to do documentation of the festival. The objectives of the project are as follows

i). Socio-cultural and political life of the Zeliangrong community have been studied particularly based on the existing secondary information. We have given a comprehensive review of literature on the community by the anthropologists, historians and colonial administrators.

ii). The documentation of the festivals of the Zeliangrong community has been done. However, the scope has been limited to oral tradition and direct interview with the knowledgeable persons and elders who organized the village level polity.

iii). The Gaan-Ngai festival as practiced among the Zeme, Liangmai and Rongmei has been studied on a worked out format.

iv). The study has examined the importance of this festival

in the present day society of the Zeliangrong people. It also examines the trend of changes that have come in the organization of the festival. It also examines the attitude of the modern day Zeliangrong people towards this festival and their cultural heritage as a whole.

Regarding the methodology, the project has adopted anthropological, historical and oral historical tools in conducting the investigation as given below:

i) The survey of the existing literatures on the history, culture, religion, polity and festivals of the three cognate groups of the Zeliangrong community of the states of Assam, Manipur and Nagaland during the colonial and post-colonial period of modern history has been done. The list of literatures needed for the subject has been enclosed in the bibliography.

ii) The following villages of the three states belonging to the three cognate groups of the Zeliangrong community have been selected for field investigation.

Assam

Lodiram, a Zeme village in Haflong, Dima Hasao District (North Cachar Hills)

Hangrum, a Zeme village in North Cachar Hills

Kaguilong, a Rongmei village of Silchar, Cachar.

Manipur

Majorkhul, a Rongmei village in Imphal West District

Thanagong, a Rongmei village in Tamenglong District

Chingmeirong, a Rongmei village in Imphal East District.

Nagaland

Kipeujang, a Zeliang village in Peren Town

Jalukie-B, a Zeliang village in Peren District

Zeliangrong village, a Rongmei village in Dimapur Town.

The study covered three states of Assam, Manipur and Nagaland, seven districts such as Dima Hasao, Cachar, Imphal West, Imphal East, Tamenglong, Peren and Dimapur and nine villages of the three cognate groups Zeme, Liangmai and Rongmei namely, Lodiram, Hangrum, Kaguilong, Majorkhul, Thanagong, Chingmeirong, Kipeujang, Jalukie-B and Zeliangrong village (Dimapur).

Two consultants for each state have been appointed who gave both written and oral information on the questionnaires and schedules supplied to them. We are also helped by a number of scholars and knowledgeable persons who supplied information on our queries. After getting information from different sources I wrote out in an approved chapterisation of the research report.

As decided earlier, the project carried out field works in the villages where the Zeliangrong Naga festivals are performed. Incidentally in the year 2012, the Gaan Ngai festival fell on 7th January in Manipur, Cachar and Dima Hasao districts of Assam. This simultaneous performance of the Gaan Ngai festival did not permit us the simultaneous field work for the festival. Therefore it was decided to carry out the field work first at Imphal town in which is located the Rongmei village of Majorkhul. It is a progressive village in an urban setting; the elders were very responsive to my research queries. Therefore I decided to carry out the intensive field work in this village. I did the participant observation of the different stages of Gaan Ngai festival from the beginning of the month when the Gaan Ngai was announced upto the end of ritual ceremonies marking the end of the festival. The daily activities of the festival were recorded by me and my research assistants through interviews with the elders and knowledgeable persons who were actively involved in carrying out the Gaan Ngai festival. Every stage and step of the festival were recorded by camera both still and live videography. On first day of Pous month of Saka era which tallies with the Manipuri month of Wakching which is officially adopted by Government of Manipur fell on 25th December 2011. The village elder announced the coming of Gaan Ngai festival. According to the notification of the Government of Manipur, Gaan Ngai started from 7th January 2012 (13th Pous or 13th Wakching of Manipur era). This date was also adopted by the Zeliangrong people of Assam both the followers of Tingkao Ragwang Chapriak cult and Heraka cult.

I interviewed several elders of the village and leaders of the boys' dormitory of Majorkhul. On the eve of Gaan Ngai which was celebrated as the festival of women folk, I interviewed respected elder named Prof. Meijinlung Kamson who was a former Member of Parliament and a Union Minister and President of the Zeliangrong Union. Since he was born and brought up in this village he gave his life time experience of the Gaan Ngai festival, working of the Village Council and village dormitories. I interviewed two elders, Gaithoachung Golmei and R. Tampikhon who were members of the village council and leaders of the women institution (Mathenmei). Since it was Gaan Ngai eve, I could meet a number of elders. Mention may be made of Abuina Golmei who is the owner of the boys' dormitory, Khangmeidun Kamei, Gaikompu Phaomei who were former leaders of the dormitory of the village. Interview with these elders are recorded in my diary and they were photographed. Thus the five days festival of Gaan Ngai in Majorkhul village is documented both by me and my research assistant, Lanchonglung Longmei.

When my research assistant is doing photography, I visited the Rongmei village of Chingmeirong and observed the festival. I interviewed an elder of the village, Kathuna Daimei who was very cooperative towards me.

While at Imphal I interviewed some scholars, namely,

K. D. Pamei who was former Joint Director of Education of Manipur and he gave information on the Liangmai festival of Chaga Ngi of Marongpa village. I also interviewed Kuije Disong of Katang village on the Zeme festivals particularly Hega Ngi. I requested an elder named Lungnihai Rongmei of Thanagong village of Khoupum valley whom I invited to visit Imphal and gave me information on the Rongmei festivals particularly Gaan Ngai. He gave information on Rongmei festivals of Tamenglong district in general and lower Rongmei of Khoupum valley.

I also requested Lanbilung Gonmei, Associate Professor of History of Imphal College of Imphal and Chaoba Kamson, General Secretary of Tingkao Ragwang Chapriak Phom to be consultants of my project. On my request they filled up the questionnaires on Gaan Ngai festival particularly of their respective villages. I interviewed both the scholars which are really helpful in my research work. Chaoba Kamson gave to me his own several publications and literatures published by Tingkao Ragwang Chapriak Phom.

After the completion of field work in Manipur, I visited Assam along with my research assistant. I visited Silchar (Kaguilong Rongmei village). I interviewed an elder of the village named Chamkandai Kamei. He volunteered to accompany me in my field work in Assam. We proceeded to Haflong in Dima Hasao district. We visited the Zeme villages of Borohaflong and Lodiram where Ramkui Newme, President of the Zeliangrong Heraka Association, North East India and Pautanzan Newme, General Secretary of the Zeliangrong Heraka Association extended full cooperation. On my earlier request they agreed to be the research consultants of the project for Assam. From Haflong we proceeded to a historic village of Hangrum in Dima Hasao district where 97th Birth Anniversary of Ranima Gaidinliu was being held. The Forest Department of Assam Government extended help to the birthday celebration of the great freedom fighter of India. I interviewed the village elders and leaders of the Zeliangrong Heraka Association at this village. Hangrum village is historically famous as it was a battle field between the armed forces of Rani Gaidinliu and Assam Rifles forces in April 1932. There is seven men Martyr Column. I had gathered rich information on Zeliangrong history, culture and particularly about the festivals during my field trip to Assam. We did recording of the oral interview and photographic documentation of the people and events. I discovered that the Zeliangrong Heraka Association performed a New Year Day on 24th January 2012 based on lunar calendar. The Zeliangrong Heraka Association is reforming the conservative Zeliangrong society towards modernity.

Then I visited Nagaland to meet a number of knowledgeable persons on the subject of my enquiry. I had earlier requested Dr. Wilubo Chawang, President of the Zeliangrong Heraka Association, Nagaland and Miss Tasile N. Zeliang, Head Mistress of Heraka Vidya Bharati School to be research consultants of the project. I met Dr. Wilubo Chawang at Dimapur and interviewed him. Then I proceeded to Jalukie-B in Peren district. I am happy to put on record that Miss Tasile N. Zeliang took the trouble of inviting several elders of Zeme and Liangmai groups at Jalukie-B and they were kind enough to give me a lot of information on Chaga Gadi (Chaga Ngi) of the Zeliang. Miss Tasile who is a writer herself with a wide experience of social and religious activities with complete mastery of both Zeme and Liangmai dialects was a mine of information for my research project. I interviewed Deralung Nren and Epelung Nring of Jalukie, Peren district on Chaga Gadi festival which was the new name of Chaga Ngi as popularisd by a section of people in Nagaland.

From Jalukie, I proceeded to Peren town, headquarter of the Zeliangrong inhabited district of Peren in Nagaland. Miss Tasile accompanied me and guided my visit to Peren. Peren is a developing town where is located. The locality of Kipeujang, the village of our field work. I was also accompanied by my mother. In Kipeujang I interviewed several elders who are the followers of the Heraka cult.

I also took photographs of the Zeme dancers. I found the Kipeujang people performing Hega Ngi. During my field visit in Nagaland, I collected some written materials on Chaga Ngi and Chaga Gadi of the Liangmai published by some scholars. I also discovered that several Christians belonging to Zeliangrong community are performing the Gaan Ngai festival or Chaga Gadi festival in Nagaland. A Rongmei group went to the extent of getting financial help from the North Eastern Zone Cultural Centre, Dimapur. In Nagaland, in Jalukie valley there are a number of Zeliangrong villages namely, Samjuram, Mhainamsi, Jalukie town, Jalukie-B where the three cognate groups namely Zeme, Liangmai and Rongmei are found living together. In Dimapur town, there are several Christian localities which perform Gaan Ngai festival in a secular way. After field work I returned to Shimla where I prepared this report on the Gaan Ngai festival of the Zeliangrong Nagas of North East India (Research and Documentation). It is a new experience for me both as a researcher and a member of the community. The following report is an outcome of my brief but intensive field work.

A statue of Rani Gaidinliu at Boro Haflong, Assam

Zeme Village of Hangrum, Assam

The author with Prof. Meijinlung Kamson at Majorkhul, Imphal

Ms Tasile N. Zeliang with the author at Jalukie-B, Nagaland

With the women folk of Kipeujang, Peren (Nagaland)

The author with Lungnihai Rongmei of Thanagong, Khoupum valley, Manipur

With some of the youths of Hangrum, Assam

2

A People with a Heroic Past

A review of literatures on Zeliangrong Nagas

The Zeliangrong which performs a well organized and well knit festival like the Gaan Ngai festival is a remarkable community. They live in the three states of Manipur, Assam and Nagaland. Zeliangrong is an acronym of the prefixes of three cognate groups of Zeme, Liangmai and Rongmei (Ze+Liang+Rong) which were adopted with the foundation of Zeliangrong Council in 1947. But historically the Zeliangrong people are an ancient tribal community of north east India who are in occupation of a compact and contiguous area which is fragmented now into the states of Assam, Manipur and Nagaland. The Zeliangrong people have a long history and a rich cultural heritage. Due to the absence of literary sources in the pre-colonial times, there were no written literatures dealing with the history, culture, religion and festivals of the Zeliangrong people. However there is rich oral tradition of the community dealing with their culture and religion. The Royal Chronicles of Manipur and the British accounts refer to the relation of the Zeliangrong community with the Meitei rulers of Manipur, the Cachari kings of Assam and the British rulers in Naga Hills and Manipur. There were several British reports and accounts dealing with the Zeliangrong community's history, culture, polity and religion during the colonial period.

The Royal Chronicle of Manipur named Cheitharol Kumbaba written in Manipuri in the ancient Meitei script along with other historical texts refer to the relation between the Manipuri rulers and the Zeliangrong people as early as the first century A.D. A historical text called Poireiton Khunthokpa (Immigration of Poireiton) in Manipuri refers to the three Naga tribes, Kabui, Tangkhul and Anal living in Manipur in the first century. The Cheitharol Kumbaba gives many references to the military conflicts between the individual Zeliangrong villages and the Meitei rulers and conquest of the Zeliangrong villages from the 12th -18th century A.D. There are also oral traditions of Zeliangrong relation with the Cachari people and their rulers. However, written accounts were left behind by the British colonial officers. The Zeliangrong was the first Naga tribe who came into contact with the British during the first Anglo-Burmese War (1824-26). Captain R.B. Pemberton of the Native Indian Infantry of the East India Company who left behind his experiences in the Narratives of the Anglo-Burmese War written by W.W. Wilson in a note on the Nagas written by Pemberton himself in 1827. He described the Zeliangrong Nagas as a fine people. He published his monumental Report on the Eastern Frontier of British India in 1835 in which he described the Rongmei Nagas relation with Raja Gambhir Singh of Manipur. But it was a British Political Agent in Manipur named Major William McCulloch who published a report named An Account of the Valley of Munnipore and surrounding Hill Tribes in 1859. McCulloch visited and intensely observed the Rongmei way of life. He however described the Rongmei tribe as Songboo. Other cognate group of the Songboo was described by him as Pooeeron meaning Puimei tribe. He also gave a linguistic table of the cognate Zeliangrong tribes. He described the Zeme as Aroong, the Liangmai as Quireng, Rongmei as Songboo and Puimei as Pooeeron. Many subsequent ethnographers including John Shakespeare could not identify the Songboo and Pooeeron.

Now a study of linguistic table of the four communities referred to by William McCulloch shows that they are from the Zeliangrong community. McCulloch described the geography, polity and culture of the Rongmeis. He described the Zeliangrong village polity as 'little republics'. Another Political Agent in Manipur named Dr. Robert Brown gives an account of the Kabuis (Rongmei and Puimei) and Koireng (Liangmai) in his report known as A Statistical Account of Manipur, 1874. For the first time Dr. Brown wrote on the religious belief and the festivals of the Rongmei Nagas. The Gaan Ngai festival was referred to as 'Enghan' festival. He also described other festivals. Brown also gave a geographical description of the land of the Zeliangrong people.

In 1885 another report entitled, The Gazetteer of Manipur was published by Captain E.W. Dun. This work of Dun referred to a large number of Rongmei, Liangmai and Puimei villages whom he described as Kabui and Kacha Naga. The famous book 'My Three Years in Manipur' written by Mrs. Ethel Grimwood in 1891 gives a reference to the southern Zeliangrong country inhabited by the Rongmei tribe and several Naga employees of the British Political Agency who belong to the Rongmeis of Imphal. The name Kabui was officially described by T.C. Hodson in his The Naga Tribes of Manipur (1911). Hodson gives a comprehensive account of the Rongmei, Puimei and Liangmai whom he called the Kabui. But the name Kabui which was of Meitei origin and referred to the Manipur chronicles was accepted as the official name of the tribe. Sir G.A. Grierson in his Linguistic Survey of India included an account of the Zeliangrong philology. Sir Grierson entrusted a Swedish scholar, Dr. Sten Konow to study the Kabui and Kacha Naga dialects of Zeliangrong language. He described the two dialects belonging to Tibeto-Burman linguistic family. He included the Zeliangrong dialects into Bodo-Naga sub-family of the Tibeto-Burman. Other Indian scholars like Dr. S.K. Chatterjee confirmed the linguistic affiliation of the Zeliangrong dialects as belonging to Tibeto-Burman family.

It was in Assam province that the British officers referred to the Zeliangrong tribe. It was E.R. Grange who published two reports on his expeditions to the Zeliangrong Naga country in his papers named 'The Narrative of an expedition into the Naga Territory of Assam' in 1938 and another paper named 'Extracts from the Journal of an Expedition into the Naga Hills on the Assam Frontier' in the Journal of Asiatic Society of Bengal. Grange reports were referred to by many writers but they did not identify the tribe of the Nagas whom Grange met. They were the Zemes of future Naga Hills district. A Superintendent of the district of Cachar named R. Steward wrote his 'Notes on Northern Cachar Hills' which was published in the Journal of Asiatic Society of Bengal in 1855. Steward refers to the Zemes as Aroong Nagas whose linguistic table was referred to by William McCulloch in his Account of 1859.

C.A. Soppit wrote 'A Short Account of the Kachcha Nagas (Empeo) Tribe in North Cachar Hills with an outline Grammar, Vocabulary and Illustrative Sentences' in 1885 published from Shillong. Soppit's account dealt with the Zeme section of the Zeliangrong community of Assam. There was certain confusion regarding the term Kachcha Nagas which in reality covered both Zeme and Liangmai. It was Sir James Johnstone, a former Political Officer of Naga Hills district of Assam and Political Agent of Manipur, who mentioned the Kachcha Nagas of Naga Hills district in his 'My Experience in Manipur and Naga Hills' published posthumously in 1896 from London. It was Sir James Johnstone and another officer named Captain John Butler who described the Zemes or Majameh of Naga Hills District as Kachcha Nagas. The two officers popularized this term. In later years the Government of Manipur adopted this term for the Zeme and Liangmai of Manipur also.

It was Sir Robert Reid, a Governor of Assam who referred to the Kachcha Nagas and Kabuis in his 'History of Frontier Areas Bordering Assam' in 1942. He refers to the rebellion of Jadonang and Gaidinliu as that of Kabuis and Kachcha Nagas. The scholars who have studied the rebellion of Jadonang and Gaidinliu described this political movement as Naga Raj Movement. Even Pandit Jawaharlal Nehru as a President of Indian National Congress wrote on the exploits of Gaidinliu in his article in Hindustan Times, 14 December 1937 entitled, 'In Surma Valley: A daughter of the Hills'. He described Gaidinliu as Queen of the Nagas (Rani). This title had struck to Gaidinliu as a freedom fighter.

In the post-colonial period, the first account on the Zemes was published by Ursula Graham Bower who wrote the Naga Path in 1950. Bower's book was a very pleasant reading account of the Zeliangrong history, economy, polity and cultural life. She was a keen observer of the Zeme life during the colonial period. However, Gangmumei Kamei was the first historian who wrote 'A History of the Zeliangrong Nagas From Makhel to Rani Gaidinliu' on a scientific historical method. This work deals with the land, history, society, religion, economy, culture and polity of the Zeliangrong people from the prehistoric times down to the present times. It was regarded by the students of history and sociology as a model for writing history of pre-literate and non-literate tribal society. Namthubuiyang Pamei wrote on this tribe in his Trail from Makuilongdi. R.K. Ringthim wrote on Odyssey A Brief account of the Zeliangrong Struggle for freedom and peace. The Zeliangrong Naga Tribe: A brief Account published by All Zeliangrong Students' Union is a brief but definitive account of Zeliangrong community. E. Zeliang's Learning the Zeliangrong Language is an important account of Zeliangrong linguistic study.

There are a lot of writings in the Zeliangrong dialects dealing with religion, history, culture and festivals of different cognate groups. R. Marulung's writings are highly commendable. Regarding the Gaan Ngai festival, there are many publications in English which are listed in the bibliography. Mention may be made of Gaan-Ngai A Festival of Zeliangrong People (Chaoba Kamson (ed), 2003) which is a collection of learned papers on Gaan Ngai festival, Philosophy of Gaan-Ngai (Chaoba Kamson, 2010), Socio-cultural and spiritual traditions of Zeliangrongs (Chaoba Kamson(ed), 2011), Gaan-Ngai Festivity among the Zeliangrong of North East India (State Level Gaan Ngai Celebration Committee, Manipur, 2012), Herakame Leu (N.C. Zeliang, 1974), Zeliangrong Heraka Movement and socio-cultural awakening in Naga society (N.C. Zeliang, 2005), Ranipuri Gaidinliu Pajat Tin Thiu Khaibo (Biography of Rani Gaidinliu in Liangmai) (Tasile N. Zeliang, 2008), Post-modern understanding of Chaga Gadi for social transformation (S.P. Tunchapbo, 2011), Heraka The Primordial Religion and its Revitalization Movement (Zeliangrong Heraka Association NEI, 2011), Zeliangrong Customary Laws (Zeliangrong Heraka Association NEI, 2009), Chagaa gadi Festival and its significance (Achenbou Nuimai, 2010), Chaga Gadi (Tunchapbo S.P. 2010).

The Ethnicity of the Zeliangrong

The word 'ethnic' comes from the Greek word 'ethno' which means a people. Zeliangrong is an ethno, a people and an ethnic group. Ethnicity is the primordial consciousness of an ethnic group in this sense; the Zeliangrong people have a primordial consciousness of belonging to an ethnic community. A tribe or ethnic community believed to be in real or imagined, common origin speaking a common language or dialects possessing common cultural traits which has a common political system with more or less similar economic system. A historian observes that it is a unique historical experience of the Zeliangrong people to force unity and brotherhood and assert their distinct identity. History and geography have been cruel to the ancestors of the Zeliangrong people in evolving a common identity. It took nearly a century of the modern times to establish the geographical space and ethnic space of their people.

It was only in 1947 that the leaders of the Zeme, Liangmai and Rongmei cognate groups coined the common name Zeliangrong. During the last 65 years, the name Zeliangrong has been used as the name of common organizations of the people in respect of community's organizations, students' organizations, women organization and religious organizations covering several religious denominations, Christian, Heraka and Tingkao Ragwang Chapriak. However the Government of India has not given recognition to the name of this collectivity. The state of Nagaland recognized them as Zeliang (Ze+Liang); Assam Government gave recognition to them as Jeme and Rongmei under the umbrella of Any Naga Tribe. The Government of Manipur recognized them as Kabui and Kacha Naga covering the Rongmei, Puimei, Zeme and Liangmai which are now recognized as separate Scheduled Tribes.

The multiplicity of names of the three cognate groups and absence of a common name for the Zeliangrong collectivity was due to confusion created by Manipur state and the British Government of Assam for using outsider names for the three cognate groups. As noted earlier, Zeme was known as Aroong Nagas in North Cachar Hills; the Zeme or Majemah was known as Kacha Nagas in Naga Hills District; the Rongmeis were known to the Meiteis of Manipur as Kabui. The Liangmai was recorded as Quireng by the British in the 19th century. In the 20th century, the Zemes of Manipur came to be known as Kacha Naga like that of Naga Hills District. Thus by the end of the 20th century Zeliangrong came to be known by different names as per the decisions of the respective state governments and as such they were recognized as Scheduled Tribe.

Yet several publications of the Government like The Scheduled Tribes published by Anthropological Survey of India and edited by Dr. K. S. Singh used the Zeliangrong collectivity to mean the Zeme, Liangmai and Rongmei of the cognate tribes of the three states. The Kohima District Gazetteer published by the Census of India and the Government of Nagaland used the common name Zeliangrong to cover Zeme, Liangmai and Rongmei. There is an ongoing pressure from different organizations of the people demanding the recognition of Zeliangrong as Scheduled Tribes in the states of Assam, Manipur and Nagaland.

The Zeliangrong Habitat and Ecology

The Zeliangrong habitat covers a compact and contiguous area namely, Tamenglong district, western Sadar Hills, Mao west and Loktak project area of Manipur state, Haflong, Herangojoa of Dima Hasao district (North Cachar Hills) of Assam and Peren district of Nagaland. Geographically the Zeliangrong territory covers the great Barail Range and its branches ranging from Dansiri river in the north and to the confines of the Chin Hills of Myanmar with Bhuvan Hills, Jiri river and Haflong plateau in the west, and the Barail watershed in the north east adjoining Angami country, the Mao Maram hills and Koubru Laimatol hill range in the east overlooking Manipur valley.

The southern boundary of the Zeliangrong area according to British ethnographers in the 19th century was at the latitude of 24.70€ N though more accurate line is 24.30€ N running across the northern Churachandpur district of Manipur touching Thangjing hills of Manipur and Bhuvan hills of eastern Cachar district of Assam. Therefore the Zeliangrong inhabited area according to a rough estimate is nearly 12,000 sq Km situated over the northern, western and southern branches of the Barail range. The steep mountains, deep gorges and the narrow river valleys have made the

Zeliangrong region physically isolated from the outside world. The important mountain peaks of the region are Mt. Paona (8,157 ft) and Mt. Angola (6,764 ft) in northern Zeliangrong territory within the state of Nagaland; the Haflong Asalu Laishong spur of western Barail; the Makuilongdi range southward from Mt. Tenipu in Mao area of northern Manipur connecting with the Koubru and Laimatol range. The main rivers of the region in Nagaland are the Dansiri river (known as Temaki), the Diphu river (Duidiki) flowing down from the Paona peak and into Dansiri, Tasangki in the west of Peren flows into the Barak river. The main rivers in Manipur sector of Zeliangrong region are the Jiri, the Makru, the great Barak, the Irang, the Ijei and the Leimatak. Other rivers are the Aling and the Dzuko bordering Manipur and Nagaland. The Jiri river is the boundary between western Zeliangrong area and the Cachar plains of Assam. The most important river is the Barak. The Barak known as Ahu or Agu or Mbeiki has been described as the 'river of rivers'. It is the largest, longest and most important river. The Barak and its tributaries are interwoven in the folklore and world view. The Zeliangrong poets, bards and singers have described the Barak river as their mother and the Irang river as the father of the people. Even the Milky Way in the sky has been poetically described as the Ahu-Arang of the universe. The Barak waterfalls which are a four step cascades is a place of great natural beauty. Mention may be made of the famous Dzuko valley which flows from the Barail watershed to the south of Puilwa (Papolongmai) and into the great Barak. There are also beautiful natural landmarks like the Barak waterfalls, the Zeilad lakes, Dzuko valley and the Khoupum valley. The Zeliangrong area has rich flora and fauna which greatly enrich the ecology and environment of the region.

Origin and migration

We do not have an authentic and scientific account of the origin of the Zeliangrong people. But the traditions recorded in the hymns and legends of the people mentioned about the cosmogony or the myth of creation of the universe, man and animals. According to a ritual hymn chanted in a rite of the worship of mother earth known as the Dichuk the myth of creation of the universe, earth and man is narrated. According to one author, "Tingkao Ragwang directed a God named Didampu and Goddess Didampui to create the earth. The two deities consulted a spider that advised that they might consult the Supreme God for His direction. As per advice of the Supreme God, the two deities directed the earthworm to excrete a sod of earth in the form of an egg which was kept hanging by a string from the space. A rat broke the string and the sod of earth fell on the water. The earthworm and Tingthinpui, an amphibious insect, which burrows underground and flies gradually, enlarged the egg size sod of clay into the earth".

"Man was also created by the will of God. The hymn of the naming ceremony (Najumgaimei) gives a myth according to which the two deities, Didampu and Didampui (Dampapui) were further advised by the Supreme God to create man, and man was created. The hymn was too short. Another tradition gives a narrative in which the two deities created several prototypes of man; they created a fish called Khagak, a toad and a monkey. The Supreme God was not pleased, so the fish was freed into the water, the toad on the land, and the monkey in the trees. Being not satisfied at the creation of the two deities, Supreme God, Tingkao Ragwang showed His image to them so that they could create man and woman after the likeliness of His image. The two deities created a man and a woman with the clay of the earth. But the two bodies were lifeless. Once again, the two deities approached the Supreme God who breathed-life-soul to the man and woman. Man was thus created. According to a belief, these two deities specially, the Goddess continues to create a child in the womb of the mother and it is she who pushes the child to the human world at the time of birth. The two deities also created plants, animals, birds and insects".

According to the legends, the birth place of the ancestors of the Zeliangrong people was known as Taobhei which was a cave out of which man and animals created by God came out to the living world. The cave has been identified with a place named Ramting Kabin which is located in a deep gorge near Makuilongdi near Wilong village in north Manipur. There is also a tradition that the ancestors of the people came from Makhel along with other Naga tribes. They migrated to Ramting Kabin and then to Chawang Phuning or Chagong Phuning where they made a settlement. Out of Chawang Phuning was developed a cluster of settlements known as Makuilongdi. From Makuilongdi the ancestors of the Zeliangrong people migrated to different direction. One group went to Niu village. They came to be known as Zeme, the inhabitants of the hinterland. This village is now known as Yangkhullen. Another group went to south and they settled down in the Koubru mountain. Another group went to Kajinglong. Those who stayed back at Makuilongdi, Kajinglong and in Koubru mountain were known as Liangmai meaning the northerners. From Makuilongdi and Kajinglong several groups migrated to the south and west, they came to be known as Rongmei (people of the southern region). There is a strong view that the name of the people who originally lived in Makuilongdi was known as Hana or Hamei. It took a number of centuries for different sections of the people to migrate to the present Zeliangrong habitat. From 18th century onwards, the Zeliangrong people migrated to Manipur valley and section of the people started settling down in Cachar valley in the beginning of the 19th century. The people still continue to migrate within and outside the Zeliangrong area till the end of the 20th century.

A Brief History

Due to the lack of sources of information it is an extremely difficult job to reconstruct the history of Zeliangrong people. It will be worthwhile to reproduce the observation of Gangmumei Kamei on the writing of history of Zeliangrong people. He says, "The concept of history as understood by historians does not exist in the vocabulary of Zeliangrong people. Their view of history is limited to the story of the past or the story of their forefathers. The term 'Theidou-Pari' or 'Nthei-Pari' means literally the story of the past and it has been used loosely to mean the myths, legends, oral traditions and actual happenings of the past. The 'Nthei-Pari' cannot meet the critical requirements of the Greek 'Historia' or the English 'History' or Sanskrit 'Itihasa'. It comes nearer to the Meitei word 'Puwari' meaning the story of forefathers...

"The past story of the Zeliangrong people is narrated in their rich folklore, myths and legends, songs and ballads, religious hymns and oral traditions handed down from generation to generation. As they are not written into texts and documents, they remain in the realm of oral folklore. However, history is regarded sometimes as the folk memory of a community, particularly of a non-literate or preliterate one, which shares the common heritage. Myth, for example, has been described as an echo or reminiscence of an incident or story that occurred in the distant past. And the Zeliangrong account of their history is abundant in their treasure house of their past traditions".

"It does not mean that the Zeliangrong view on their past is equivalent to history as generally understood by the historians. But it is a fact that every community including the Zeliangrong people has definitely an ancient past, their origin, migration, struggle for sustenance, victory, defeat and glory. We may refer to what Dr. E.B. Tylor said long ago about the tribal tradition; 'What they relate is fiction and what they mention is history'. We need not necessarily apply the critical scrutiny or test to their folklore, and we may not accept whatever is narrated. The historian cannot write history without the sources of information; without that he will be a mere storyteller. It is contingent on the historian to broaden the range of his sources of information, not necessarily confining himself to the archaeological evidence, literary work, written documents and the archival records... Therefore, for writing the history of a people like the Zeliangrongs who have passed through the evolution and development of their society, culture and civilization from the stage of the 'caveman' to the Old Stone Age (Paleolithic), and the Neolithic and to the formation of political organization and social institutions, practice of agriculture, experience of the tribal stage of social development or contact with developed civilizations like the Manipuri, Kachari and the British, the usual method of historiography can be utilized" (Gangmumei Kamei, A History of the Zeliangrong Nagas from Makhel to Rani Gaidinliu, 2004, pp. 19-20).

Within this concept a brief historical account of the Zeliangrong people will cover the legendary and pre-historical period, pre-colonial period, colonial period and post-colonial period.

The Zeliangrong Society

The Zeliangrong society like the Naga society is a well-knit society based on kinship structure. The Zeliangrong community is divided into clans and the clan hood is the basis of the evolution of the social institutions of the community. According to tradition, the ancient people attended a common dormitory along with gods. A patriarch deity known as Tingpurengsonang presided over the dormitory. Due to mistrust, suspicion and conflict between man and gods, Tingpurengsonang decided separation between man and gods and the two were made invisible. The first clan is referred to the legend of the great lawgiver known as Amang or Amangbou. The lawgiver is said to have belong to Pamei clan and his clan was known as Amang Puina Pamei (Pamei the descendent of Amang). Despite this mythical reference to Pamei clan, historically the Zeliangrong society was organized into clans and lineages, even in sub-lineages. Originally when the ancestors of the Zeliangrong people were living in Makuilongdi village, there were two main clans where they developed a culture based on a settled agriculture with an organized political system and functional religion. The archaeological evidence of two megaliths known as 'Pamei Tao' (Pamei megalith) and 'Newmei Tao' (Newmei megalith) having discovered in the site of ancient Makuilongdi indicates the existence of two phratries (clans?), the Pamei and the Newmei. We may believe that originally there were only two clans, the Pamei and Newmei. Later on several lineages were developed among the cognate groups of Zeme, Liangmai and Rongmei. There are two clans which originated from Yangkhullen known as Hau and Heu which are equivalent with Pamei and Newmei. Several Zeme villages in Nagaland follow this Hau and Heu whereas the Zemes of Assam and Manipur adopt Pamei and Newmei. These two clans, Pamei and Newmei are found among the three cognate groups as indicated below.

The Zeliangrong Clans

Clan.	*Zeme*	*Liangmai*	*Rongmei*	*Totem*
Pamei	Pame	Pamei	Pamei/Mpamei/ Kamei	Ahuina bird (green pigeon)
Newmei	Newme (Hnume)	Newmei	Newmei	Loingao bird (Shrike)
Daimei	Ndaime	Daimei	Daimei	Ahuina bird (green pigeon)
Riamei	Riame	Maremmei	Riamei/ Remmei	Frog

Liangmai Clans

The Liangmai had developed several clans and lineages as given below.

1. Pamei
2. Newmei
3. Daimei
4. Maremmei
5. Remmei
6. Malangmei

Zeme Clans

The Zeme had two major clans and several lineages

1. Npame (Pamei)
2. Newme (Hnume)
3. Nkuame
4. Nriame
5. Ndaime
6. Sogame
7. Hezame

Rongmei Clans

Pamei or Kamei lineages	Newmei lineages	Other clans
1. Pamei	1. Newmei	1. Gangmei
2. Kamei	2. Riamei (Remmei)	2. Rongmei
3. Phaomei	3. Daangmei/Danghangmei	
4. Malangmei	4. Panmei	
5. Kamson	5. Thaimei	
6. Siangongmei	6. Gonmei	
7. Thaankang	7. Gonthangmei	
8. Daimei	8. Maringmei	
9. Khandangmei		
10. Ngaomei		
11. Khongmei		
12. Daimei		

The Ranked Society

The traditional Zeliangrong society is a ranked society. There was an age and sex gradation. The Zeliangrong people are divided into the above mentioned gradation. For example, the Zemes are graded in the ranks based on age.

(i) Ngeka (babyhood)

(ii) Hemanka (childhood)

(iii) Hengname (adolescence)

(iv) Rehangba (Young buck)

(v) Hengluime (married man)

(vi) Hepeu (between 45-55 when procreation is normally over)

(vii) Kaching (elderly group= who qualify for the membership of the village council, Samkakibe)

(viii) Chipaume (oldest group: Ting Kupeu, engaged in priestly activities)

Other cognate groups also follow more or less same system.

The Dormitory System

The dormitory is an important social institution, which sustains the Zeliangrong society, religion and culture. We do not know the origin of the institution. Functional analysis shows that the dormitory meets the educational needs of the young men and young women; it also meets the defence requirement of the village and the manpower requirement to organize public works, religious ceremonies and cultural festivals including dance and music. The dormitory was perhaps evolved to meet these needs of the people. And now when these requirements are met many modern schools and government development departments of the state, this institution obviously dies. But it exists among the people who follow the traditional indigenous religion.

The membership of the dormitory in a village was compulsory for the boys and girls at the time of reaching puberty. The boys when they reached pre-puberty stage (9-10 yrs) started sleeping in the boy's dormitory. Even married men slept in the dormitory though after marriage, the male may not sleep there as a compulsion. For a female the membership of the girls' dormitory ceased with her marriage when she would sleep in her husband's house. Her husband would continue to be a member of the dormitory. This membership is very important. There may have been one or more than two dormitories. These were traditions of seven male dormitories and seven female dormitories. This membership of the dormitory is known as Kienga in Zeme and Thien in Liangmai and Rongmei. Ursula Graham Bower in her well known account of the Zeme Nagas (Naga Path, 1950) writes, that she was admitted to a dormitory and her Kienga helped her in many organizations though as an unmarried girl, her role in the dormitory was limited.

Functions

The dormitory's functions are:

(i) to serve as a communal sleeping hall for the boys and other members of the dormitory;

(ii) to impart traditional education, warfare and art of fighting by the use of weapons, dance, music, art and crafts, customs, traditions and folklore to the younger members;

(iii) to act as a guard house for the defence of the village. Such warriors are known as Riphen. Protection of the lives of the men, women and children is sometimes taken up by strong individual warrior heroes known as Liangtong.

(iv) to act as a centre of cultural activities. The festivals and ceremonies for the village or individuals are organized by the dormitory. The dormitory renders services for the individual households or village council during the time of marriage and other social occasions.

(v) to construct paths, and clean ponds in and around the village.

The dormitory inculcates in the young men and young women a strong sense of fraternity and corporate life in the village, which is essential for sustaining the tribal community life. In modern times, it has declined but it still serves to perform its social, religious and cultural functions of the village. Where there is no dormitory, its function has been taken by the youth clubs and organizations. Above the dormitory, the elder's house, the Gaanchang is very important. Those who have gone through the experiences of the gradation in the dormitory are promoted to Gaanchang. They are now equipped to be the members of the village council, Pei or Samkakibe and hold offices. Above them the Banjas perform the religious functions.

Above the girl's dormitory, there is the women's house, Mathenmei of which all the married women of the village are members. Their functions are limited but they perform some social functions during festivals and religious ceremonies. Above Mathenmei is the Kengjapui (old women's group), assigned with ritual functions during births, deaths and religious ceremonies.

Thus, we find that the Zeliangrong society at the village level is well organized through sex and age grades. The social hierarchy is not based on economic classes, but on what has just been described.

The Zeliangrong Polity

The Zeliangrong polity is based on the village which is a distinct unit of political and social importance. The political, social, economic and religious life is regulated by the village polity. Gerontocracy with a democratic ethos is the nature of the Zeliangrong polity. The Zeliangrong people did not develop a tribe or community level polity formation. The political and administrative structure is based on the pattern of ownership of the lands within the village. The clans, lineages and sub-lineages are given functionary position both executive and judicial. At times the Zeliangrong polity has a strong element of theocracy. The priest-administrator occupies a high position and his ecclesiastical function controls the whole administration of the village. He is regarded as the head of the village council. The social and religious functions are controlled by him. The Zeliangrong polity has dual functions – secular and religious. The secular functionaries are the Kadepeo or Nampou who deal with general administration, judicial and social affairs. The ecclesiastical functionaries are Tingku, Tingkiupeu or Taku who deal with the religious affairs. This dual control in the secular and ecclesiastical affairs exercise by the village polity is the basic feature of the Zeliangrong polity. Historically, the Zeliangrong people had developed different stages of social formation. When they were migrating from Makhel to Ramting Kabin and to Chawang Phuning then to Makuilongdi, the Zeliangrong people were living in a state of a band led by a leader. The leader of the band assumes a pre-chieftanship status as indicated by the word Chawang which means a chief. So at the original villages of Chawang Phuning and Makuilongdi, the head of the polity assume the title of Chawang (king or chief). Nguiba, the chief of Makuilongdi send out migrating people under the leadership of his brothers. At Makuilongdi, the office of the chiefship had become hereditary. And according to historians all the paraphernalia of a polity was developed at Makuilongdi. Though there was a chief at Makuilongdi, it did not develop into chiefdom. Therefore the Zeliangrong polity was confined to a village polity only.

Village Council

The whole administration of the village is managed by a council which is known as Pei or Samkakibe. One British officer of North Cachar Hills described the Pei as the Council of the elders. The Pei is not only a council of elders but also the collective supreme body in which all the heads or representatives of the clans, lineage are represented. The Pei is represented by the Chief of the village who was a founder or who belonged to the founder's clan of the village. Ursula Graham Bower observes on the polity of the Zeliangrong people, "The Zeme tribal polity still survived in surprisingly complete form. When the Zeme arrived and picked on settlement, each had a leader and with this leader had been a lieutenant. In nine out of ten he was a man of other exogamous group (the Zeme had only two) and probably the leader's brother-in-law or a similar connection by marriage....

"Each community was ruled by a village council with the Kadepeo as its head. He was in effect, its President. He convened it, and with the help of the village priest, the other permanent member, chose elders to sit on it at any given meeting. But he was no dictator" (Graham Bower, The Naga Path, 1950).

We find the same system among the Liangmai and Rongmei sections. While the founder of the village who is called Nampou exist among the lower Liangmai and Rongmei; the Kadepeo is among the western Zemes and the Hankia is among the upper Zemes.

Functionaries of the Village Council

Among the western Zeme in Manipur and Assam, there are four secular functionaries and four religious affairs.

1. Kadepeo, the headman, a junior head man and two assistants.

2. Tingkupeo, the chief priest, junior priest and two assistants.

Among the upper Zeme in Nagaland, there are three functionaries

1. Hankia, head man or chief of the village
2. Hegwang, deputy chief of the village
3. Tingkupeo

Among the Liangmai, there are the following functionaries

1. Tingku, chief priest
2. Tingku kiakza, assistant to the priest
3. Nampou, owner of the village

Among the upper Rongmei in Tamenglong district, the following functionaries exist

1. Nampou, chief of the village
2. Maisinpou, who is incharge of fire
3. Raangdingpou, gate keeper
4. Maanh, blacksmith
5. Muh (Tingku), priest cum healer

Among the lower Rongmeis in southern Tamenglong, the following functionaries exists

1. Nampou, head man
2. Taku, chief priest
3. Nammu, in-charge of agricultural rites
4. Pei Kume, member of the village council from the age group of Baanjah and Gaanchang
5. Changloi, advisor-assistants

Functions of the village council

The village council is responsible for the administration of the whole affairs of the village; maintaining social cohesion, deciding on the areas for jhum cultivation, dates for the different stages of agricultural operations, announcing the gennas (abstention from work for prayer to the God) and enforcing it, punishing the violation of the gennas. The council collects rents from the tillers of the agricultural fields fro transmission to the land owners. It decides on both religious and secular matters. The authority of the council as noted above is based on the customs and the Council enforces the customary laws. The village council has the authority to decide on any vital matter and their decisions become law in the village. In course of time, it assumes the form of the customary law. However, the village council seldom deviates from the general customary laws of the community dealing with the law of person and property or religious matters.

Zeliangrong Ethnolinguistics

The present status of the three cognate groups shows that they don't have a common language. However, the three dialects have common linguistic roots. The following account of the Zeliangrong ethno linguistic is reproduced from the Brief Account of Zeliangrong Nagas prepared by All Zeliangrong Students Union in 2009, "The ancestors of the Zeliangrong people spoke a common language, which is spoken by the Liangmai today, the original core group. Philologists and linguists after a careful examination of the Zeliangrong dialects have arrived at a definite conclusion of the affinity of the dialects. Dr. G.A. Grierson, Chief Editor of the monumental Linguistic Survey of India entrusted Dr. Sten Konow, a Swedish philologist who was associated with the survey to study the language of the Zeliangrong group. Dr. Sten Konow collected the specimens of the words of the dialects of Kacha Naga (Zeme and Liangmai) and Kabui (Rongmei) with the help of knowledgeable officials of Government of Manipur in the beginning of the 20th century. Dr. Sten Konow's findings were published by Dr. Grierson in the reports of the Linguistic Survey of India, Vol.

III and Part II. It was identified that Kacha Naga and Kabui (Zeme, Liangmai and Rongmei) along with other tribes like the Maram and Koirao (Thangal) belong to the Naga-Bodo sub family of the Tibeto-Burman linguistic group. The survey also found that there was a close affinity between the Zeliangrong languages with the Bodo language of Assam. Hence they named it as the Naga-Bodo sub family".

"After Grierson, a well known Indian philologist, Dr.S.K. Chatterjee also arrived at the same conclusion. He published his finding in his famed book, Kirata Jana Kriti: The Contribution of the Indo-Mongoloid to the Indian Culture (1950). Dr. Chatterjee writes that the Kacha Naga and Kabui belong to the Naga-Bodo sub family of the Indo-Mongoloid group by race and language. Indo-Mongoloid was a term coined by Dr. Chatterjee himself. During the course of long years of migration and settlement in different regions, the three cognate groups developed dialects with local variations. Now the Zeliangrong people are speaking three dialects with common roots".

"Recently, linguistic experts from the Central Institute of Indian Languages, Mysore studied the grammar and phonology of the three dialects. They endorsed the findings of Dr. Grierson and Dr. Chatterjee regarding the Zeliangrong linguistic affinity. They identified 29 phonemes in the Zeliangrong language and dialects, common to the three dialects".

"Zeliangrong folk songs and ritual hymns are mostly sung in Liangmai dialect and in the improvised forms from region to region and village to village. And the people realize the commonness of the roots of the dialects. Recently, Elungkiebe Zeliang, a Lecturer in the Department of History of Christianity in the Eastern Theological College Jorhat, wrote a book entitled, "Learning Zeliangrong Dialects with English" in 2004 which was published by the All Zeliangrong Students' Union (AMN)".

"His study was based on the comparative examination of 1000 basic words of the Zeme, Liangmai and Rongmei dialects with English in 29 categories. He also deals with the basic grammar of the dialects and conversation practiced on eight categories of expression. Elungkiebe's study reveals the common origin of the dialects which have developed some variants which are quite natural in an unwritten language. He said, 'Today the Zeliangrong Naga speaks slightly varied dialects namely, Northern Zeme, Southern Zeme, Liangmai and Rongmei. Inspite of variations, the fact remained till today many words are common to all'. He writes, 'They have a common ancestry being descendants of same ancestors who dispersed from Makuilongdi village. This is our common tradition which we can't undo or reverse; and it is this common history that binds the Zeliangrong people together'. Elungkiebe's study has clearly confirmed the affinity of the Zeliangrong dialects".

"The growth and development of the written literatures of the three dialects has led to the transformation of the three dialects to the status of language and literature in recent times. But it does not negate the common origin and commonality of the three dialects. The independent linguistic studies confirm the ethnic and linguistic affinity of the Zeliangrong people".

"Identification of a tribe is also based on the common language. However, a tribe may have a language or several dialects. For example, the Ao tribe who speaks the dialects of Chongli and Mongsen is recognized as a single tribe. The Tangkhul who have separate dialects for every village is also a tribe. The Chakhesang tribe of Nagaland is a classic example of the formation of the tribe on the combination of the three groups, Chakhru, Kheza and Sangtam. Chakhesang is the acronym, like the Zeliangrong, with the prefixes of Chakhru, Kheza and Sangtam (Cha+Khe+Sang = Chakhesang). So the use of three dialects is no bar to a common nomenclature for the Zeliangrong people. Therefore, under the acronym of Zeliangrong as the tribe's nomenclature, Zeme, Liangmai and Rongmei continue to be the dialects or language spoken by the members of the Zeliangrong community".

The Anti-Colonial Struggle

The Zeliangrong Nagas came under the British rule in the 19th century. However, the Nagas as a whole resisted the British interference which led to conflict between the Nagas and the British. The first expedition to the Zeme area was carried out by E.R. Grange, Assistant Principal Assistant of Nowgong District. The British conquered the Zeliangrong area and established the headquarter of the Naga Hills district at the Zeme village of Asalu and one Lt. Gregory was appointed as the first Deputy Commissioner of Naga Hills district since 1866. The headquarter was shifted to Samagudting, the present Chumukedima and later on to Kohima in 1878. And 23 Zeliangrong villages were brought under the British rule. Thus in Assam, Zeliangrong areas came under the British rule.

British Conquest of Manipur, 1891

The British came to know of the Zeliangrong people living in the western hills of Manipur during the first Anglo-Burmese war. As per agreement between the East India Company and the King of Manipur, the present subdivision of Taosem inhabited by the Zeliangrong Nagas was transferred to Manipur in 1833. It was also agreed upon that the Cachar road from Silchar to Bishenpur in Imphal valley via Oinamlong, Nungba, Khoupum, Leimatak and Leimaton was constructed with the free labour provided by the Zeliangrong villagers in 1839. The British conquered Manipur in 1891 and all the hill tribes of Manipur including Zeliangrong were brought under the British administration. They were compelled to pay hill house tax.

There were several anti-British movements in colonial Manipur namely the Women Agitation of 1904, the Kuki Rebellion of 1917-1919 and the Naga Raj movement of 1930-32 under the leadership of Haipou Jadonang and Rani Gaidinliu. Haipou Jadonang started the Naga Raj movement against the British. He was imprisoned in Tamenglong in 1928 for predicting the end of the British Raj and coming of the Naga Raj. After his release he made preparation for a civil disobedience movement for realizing the Naga Raj. He was arrested in 1931 and hanged at Imphal on 29th August, 1931. Rani Gaidinliu (1915 – 1993) took up the leadership of the Naga Raj movement. She went underground and fought against the British. She was arreted in October 1932 from Puilwa village in Naga Hills district and sentenced to life imprisonment. Pandit Jawaharlal Nehru when he was the President of the Indian National Congress came to know of the Zeliangrong people's movement. He described her as the Rani of the Nagas in 1937. The Zeliangrong people of Naga Hills and Manipur continued to fight against the British even after the imprisonment of Gaidinliu. After the World War II the Zeliangrong people became aware of the impending British departure from India. On 15th February 1947 the Zeme, Liangmai and Rongmei leaders of Manipur and Naga Hills of Assam formed the Zeliangrong Council. The coining of the ethnonym, "Zeliangrong" was one of the greatest achievement of the Zeliangrong people in the 20th century.

The Zeliangrong People in Contemporary History

The Zeliangrong people of Manipur participated in the democratic process in Manipur (1948-49). They elected two MLAs to Manipur State Legislative Assembly in 1948. After the merger of Manipur with Indian Union (1949), the Zeliangrong leaders participated in the political process of Manipur. They elected a member to the electoral college of Manipur. They elected two members to the Manipur

Territorial Council in 1957 and MLAs to the Assembly. In the Naga Hills, the Zeliangrong people joined the Naga National movement since its inception. A Zeliangrong leader signed in the memorandum to the Simon Commission in 1929. The Zeliangrong leaders took active role in the formation of the Naga Peoples' Convention (1957-59). After statehood of Nagaland in 1963, Zeliangrong leaders became MLAs and Ministers. One was elected as the Member of Parliament. In Assam, the Zeliangrong people participated in the North Cachar Hills District Autonomous Council to which the Zeliangrong people elected three members. In Manipur, two Zeliangrong leaders were elected to the Parliament. One of them became a Union Minister.

The common identity of the Zeliangrong people as an ethno-cultural entity is based on the following features.

1. Common origin and history
2. Ethnic and linguistic affinity
3. Common social structure based on kinship and lineage
4. Cultural homogeneity, and
5. Common political system.

Zeliangrong Dancers in 1887 reproduced from Julian Jacobs, 1990

Martyrs Column of the Battle of Hangrum, 1932

3

A Community of Spirituality

A critique of Animism

Following Sir E.B. Tylor who was the first professor of Social Anthropology in Cambridge University, anthropologists, Christian missionaries and tribal elites had accepted the stigmatic animism to describe the religious belief of the tribal people in the 19th century who were described as savages. Sir E.B. Tylor in his classic, "Primitive Culture; researches into development of Mythology, Philosophy, Religion, Art and Culture" published in 1871 describes animism as the definition of religion of the savage as the belief in Spiritual Being. His critics pointed out that Tylor's use of the term, animism as misleading. Animism is a belief that all natural objects have souls but Tylor's animism is more a spiritism, worship of spirits which deals with the unempirical world of the spirits. The critics particularly Andrew Lang and Emile Durkheim observed that "the belief in spiritual beings (soul, ghost and demon) did not cover the primitive religion or the religious beliefs of the tribal". Andrew Lang (1844-1912) theorized that the primitive tribes believed in a High God, a creator of the Universe, and a Supreme God. He pleaded that there was a belief in primordial monotheism. E.B. Tylor dismissed this as an imagination of the Christian missionaries. Another German philosopher in his "Origin of the idea of God" (1912) pointed out that in the primitive religion there was a concept of high God and he confirmed primordial monotheism of Andrew Lang.

But the great prestige of E.B. Tylor was universally accepted. In India the government administrators including ethnographers were instructed by the then British Government of India to use the term animism to describe the religion of the tribals or the indigenous communities. In north east India the newly established Directorate of Ethnography under the Assam Government instructed the writers dealing with the anthropological monographs to describe the tribal religions as animism. Following these anthropological writers Christian missionaries adopted terms like heathen, pagan and animism. The tribal religion was condemned as a worship of demons and evil spirits. Even the tribal educated elite including the Christian converts accepted this description of their religion as animism. However, enlightened scholars of tribal communities who are the followers of indigenous religion refused to accept this derogatory name. Even Christian writers who have sympathy for the tribal culture do not accept such a name.

However, no scholar could challenge E.B. Tylor's theory of animism. In 2006 a Naga historian, Gangmumei Kamei published his landmark "Essays on Primordial Religion" which is a collection of four essays on the religion of the tribes. He published a sensational paper named Primordial Religion: defining the tribal religion. This was originally a paper read at the national seminar on the indigenous religions of North- east India organized by the Centre for Study of Civilization, New Delhi. In his paper he quoted Dr. Harold Turner, a Presbyterian theologian of New Zealand who came out in a strong defence of religion of the indigenous people. He declared that the tribal people do not like to be called heathen, savage, primitive or superstitious and words like animism, preliterate etc. Turner argued that instead of animism the word primal religion should be adopted to describe the tribal religion. He gave six features of primal religion. Professor Gangmumei Kamei observes that animism is an inaccurate and fallacious name for the religion of the indigenous people. He however endorses some of the tenets of primal religion to be inclusive within the tribal religion. He proposes the term primordial religion to describe the tribal religion. His observation on the affinities and differentiation between primal religion and primordial religion is worth reproducing. Primordial religion according to him comes from the word primordial which means literally "existence since the beginning of time".

"The primal religion covers all the features of the indigenous faith or the tribal religion. An indigenous faith implies an ancient root and cultural heritage, the present consciousness and future continuance. The term 'prior to the universal religion' expresses the ancient but do not necessarily represent the present status and the future. Many Indian scholars and Hindu philosophers have described Hinduism as 'Sanatan Dharma' which has been interpreted as an ancient and eternal religion or way of life. Likewise applying the criteria of antiquity and eternity, the indigenous tribal religion has been also described as Sanatan Dharma, not in the sense of Hinduism but on the basis of similarity of the tribal religion with Hinduism.

"We find the similarity in essence to indigenous faith with some popular form of Hinduism. Therefore it is thought that the more appropriate term to describe the indigenous tribal faith is 'Primordial religion' meaning a religion with a primordial existence; existing since the beginning of time. Primordiality is basic to any religion which is based on a myth of creation which ascribes to the Supreme Being as the Creator of the Universe, men and all living beings. Ivar Lissner, a German scholar in his book, 'Man, God and Magic' (1961) used the term 'primordial religion'. On the empirical level, an overview of the indigenous religions of the major tribal communities of north east India shows that they have a common feature of polytheism with a strong belief in the Supreme God, the creator and the Almighty God. These tenets meet all the essentialities of a functional religion with a philosophy and theology. The primordial religious system has the following features.

1. Belief in the Supreme God who is the creator of the Universe, benevolent and protector of men.
2. Belief in the existence of many gods and deities who are to look after the different aspects of the world, nature and humans.
3. The concept of Ancestor worship and belief in the rebirth of soul.
4. Belief in the Heaven, the abode of God and gods; land of the Dead where the man or his soul goes after death.
5. Belief in the deities presiding over villages and places.
6. Offerings made to gods and deities in the worship or propitiation to them.
7. The performance of the Rites of Passage, festivals of the community and individual ceremonies.
8. Organisation of the religion at the village levels.
9. Concept of sin as a deviation from social and moral code and customs, and retribution by God, society and man for the sin.
10. Belief in the redemption and salvation of soul for the good doers
11. Traditionally, the tribal religions have no founders; they are historically evolved. They do not usually have any name.

"The recent trend in the primordial religion is the establishment of religious organizations which supervise their ancient religion. They have coined name or discovered ancient name for their religion. The village level religion has been upgraded to community level. They have written down the religious teachings and tenets in books in their own dialects. There is a concurrent development of religion and culture. Religion is seen as an aspect of cultural heritage and social solidarity. Leaders of the religion have developed philosophy and theology in their own way.

"They give strong emphasis that primordial religion and culture are inseparable. Culture can be preserved when the religion of the community survives. There is a universal realization of the identity of the indigenous people who are aroused to fight for the preservation of their religion and culture" (Gangmumei Kamei, Essays on Primordial Religion, 2006, pp.15-17)

Revitalization of Indigenous Faiths

The British conquest of north east India heralded the advent of Christian missions and the conversion of the tribal people into Christianity like the Garos, the Khasis, the Naga, the Kuki, the Mizo and other. As noted in previous paragraphs, the Christian missionaries condemned the indigenous religion and culture. However, while many indigenous tribes were converted into Christianity, the enlightened section of the indigenous faiths started the movement for reform or revitalization of their religious beliefs. During the colonial period there were several religious reformers; namely U Jeebon Roy of the Khasis, Jadonang and Rani Gaidinliu among the Zeliangrong Nagas, Naoria Phulo, a Meitei thinker who tried to revitalized Meitei Sanamahi religion and among the Bodos of Assam, Gurudev Kalicharan Brahma started the revitalization movement. In the post colonial period, it was Talom Rukbo, an Adi scholar of Arunachal Pradesh who organized a traditional faith known as Donyi-Polo. There are religious traditions like Rangfraism among the Tangsas of Changlang district of Arunachal Pradesh, Nunna Lalchhunga

Kua among the Mizo and Bathowism among the Bodos, and the Lhikeri among the Chakhesang Nagas of Nagaland.

Zeliangrong Religious Movement

Of all these movements we take up the Zeliangrong religious movement. This movement under the leadership of Haipou Jadonang and Rani Gaidinliu was a comprehensive tribal millenarian movement. It was the reaction against the British colonial rule. It aimed at the liberation from the colonial rule, social integration of all cognate tribes of the Zeliangrong Naga covering the Zeme, Liangmai and Rongmei and religious reforms and cultural resurgence. Apart from the political objective of a Naga Raj, the social and religious reforms are of far reaching consequences. The revitalization of the Zeliangrong religion and culture was the main theme of the movement. The colonial authorities looked at this movement as a rebellion against the British and the Christians looked at it as an anti Christian heather movement. The reform movement was definitely not against the Christians or Christianity. The Christian constituted a microscopic minority in the Zeliangrong population in the late 1920's. The leader of the movement was Haipou Jadonang.

Religious Legacy of Jadonang (1905-1931)

"The religious legacy of Jadonang was his religious reforms in the traditional and orthodox Zeliangrong religion and society. His reforms were a synthesis of religious monotheism with idolatory and temple culture, simplied and rationalized form of religious worship leading towards social and religious solidarity among the Zeliangrong people reviving the common past and origin" (Gangmumei Kamei, Essays on Primordial Religion, 2006). Jadonang's contribution was the emphasis on the worship of the Supreme God, Tingkao Ragwang (or Tingwang) in rational form, community and individual worship of God for welfare and prosperity. The worship consists of prayer, ritual dances, ritual hymns and sacrifices. He insisted on an individual devotion and prayer to Tingkao Ragwang with "folded hands" facing the east. His abolition of the taboos and gennas had purified the traditional religion without deviating from the essence of the Zeliangrong religion. He composed hymns and ritual dances as revealed by God. His two temples showed some outward influence of church architecture and Hindu idolatory. There are two trends in his legacy; one is sporadic and unorganized link with the traditional religion and the other is the innovative and organized form of a reformed cult which was, after thirty years, named Heraka by his follower and disciple, the legendary freedom fighter, Rani Gaidinliu. In their last pilgrimage to the holy cave of God Bisnu, Tingkao Ragwang revealed a set of religious beliefs and practices which formed the essence of the Heraka cult (See Gangmumei Kamei's Jadonang: A Mystic Naga rebel).

The Heraka Cult

After Haipou Jadonang's martyrdom in 1931 and imprisonment of Rani Gaidinliu, the religious movement of the Zeliangrong people continued in two streams. The indigenous faith continued to be followed by the Zeliangrong people and Rani Gaidinliu started a religious cult known as Heraka. She became the patron saint of the Heraka religion. We discuss the philosophy and theology of Heraka cult in a subsequent paragraph. However, we give a brief account of this cult.

Heraka literally means "Pure" in Zeme. Therefore according to Rani Gaidinliu, Heraka religion is the essence of Zeliangrong belief as revealed by Tingkao Ragwang or Tingwang. "The Heraka believes in Tingwang, the Supreme God who is the cause or the root of all creation, the creator of the universe. He is good and benevolent and is worship by all. The belief in the worship of one Supreme God by Heraka is based on a concept of monotheism. The Heraka does not worship smaller gods and deities. The mode of worship is very simple. It is in the form of prayer at the individual or community congregation singing the hymns in the praise of Tingwang. They worship Tingwang on full moon day which is known as Bupu-Ngai (festival of the full moon). Rani Gaidinliu, the patron-saint composed appropriate hymns and dances for such auspicious occasion. Heraka had simplified the rites of birth, marriage and death. It is a reform monotheistic religion".

Emergence of Tingkao Ragwang Chapriak (TRC)

Another legacy of Haipou Jadonang is the practice of religious pilgrimage to the holy caves of God Bisnu in the Bhuvan Hills in Cachar district of Assam. It is believed that God Bisnu used to communicate through priests and diviners on the religious teaching and practice of the Zeliangrong people. The followers of the traditional faith started making annual congregation and pilgrimages to this holy caves. A temple of God Bisnu was constructed. In March 1993, a meeting of the Zeliangrong community leaders of the states of Manipur, Assam and Nagaland was held at Bhuvan hills to discuss the future of the Zeliangrong religion. They organized first conference on Zeliangrong religion at Imphal on 14-16 April 1994. The conference after three days of deliberation founded the Zeliangrong Religious Council to act as a sole authority of the Zeliangrong religion. The conference also declared the name of the Zeliangrong religion to be christened as "Tingkao Ragwang Chapriak" (Religion of Tingkao Ragwang). It was pronounced at the ceremony of Laogai Karikmei (holding the holy iron hoe in the name of God).

The two religious streams, the Heraka and Tingkao Ragwang Chapriak popularly known by its abbreviation, TRC are two complementary traditions of the Zeliangrong religion; the first is monotheistic and the second is polytheistic with strong emphasis on Supreme God. Both Tingwang of the Heraka and Tingkao Ragwang of TRC are the one and same Divinity. The TRC maintains the traditional system but abolished all unnecessary taboos like unnatural deaths and gennas like the Heraka. Both have appeared as refined and rational theology and philosophy. TRC is a historically evolved religion while Heraka is a revealed religion with the tenets of Zeliangrong religion.

Philosophy of Zeliangrong Religion

Since its foundation in 1994, the Zeliangrong Religious Council later on renamed as Tingkao Ragwang Chapriak Phom published a large number of religious tracts explaining the philosophy of Tingkao Ragwang Chapriak. Among their publications mention may be made of their authoritative text on "Rites of Passage" known as "Ringlon Theilon" published in 2002. They also published several editions of devotional songs and hymns since 2002. They also published a tract entitled, "Tingkao Ragwang Chapriak: The Zeliangrong primordial Religion" in 2005 which was rendered into English by Gangmumei Kamei. This tract contains 10 sections which constitute the theology and philosophy of Tingkao Ragwang Chapriak (TRC).

The Concept of Tingkao Ragwang Chapriak

"Zeliangrong religion is now known as the Tingkao Ragwang Chapriak. It was named after the Supreme God worshipped by the Zeliangrong from time immemorial. Tingkao Ragwang or Tingwang means the Heavenly God, the Supreme God. So Tingkao Ragwang Chapriak means the religion of Tingkao Ragwang".

"The religion had no name. And once upon a time the religion of the tribal people was described by the western scholars as 'Animism' which means belief in spiritual beings, the spirits, ghosts and demons. This is a mistaken notion.

The fallacy of animism has been exposed to be an invalid concept. Now terms like primal religion, primeval religion and primordial religion have been proposed by the scholars of philosophy and theology. Of these the primordial religion appears to be more accurate and appropriate to define the indigenous tribal religion including the Zeliangrong religion.

Primordial Religion

Primordial religion means a religion with a primordial existence, existing since the beginning of time, ancient and eternal. It is almost equivalent to Sanskrit word "Sanatan Dharma" meaning an ancient and eternal religion. Tingkao Ragwang Chapriak is thus a primordial religion of the Zeliangrong people, a religion practiced and followed by them since the creation. However, the Tingkao Ragwang Chapriak is polytheism, a religion which worships many gods, goddesses and deities though it gives great emphasis to the worship of the Supreme God. It has henotheistic features and it believes in the Supreme God as the highest God out of many gods.

Tingkao Ragwang Chapriak has the following tenets of a primordial religion.

1. Belief in Supreme God, Tingkao Ragwang who is the creator of the universe, gods and men, who is benevolent and protector of men. He is omniscient, omnipresent and omnipotent.
2. Belief in the existence of many gods and deities who are assigned by the Heavenly God to look after the different aspects of the world, nature and humans.
3. Belief in the concept of heaven, the abode of God, Tingkao Ragwang Kai or Tingkao Kaidai and the life after death represented by the land of the dead where man's soul goes after death.
4. Belief in the worship of the deities presiding over the

villages and places (Shong and Bambu) to act as the guardian deities of men in these villages.

5. Belief in the concept of the ancestor worship (Kairao Kalummei) and in the concept of the rebirth of the human soul.
6. Worship of Gods (Ra Kalummei) and propitiation of lower deities (Ra Khaangmei)
7. Belief in the concept of sin which is known as "Non" as deviation or violation of the religious, moral and social customs and norms and retribution by God for the same.
8. Belief in the performance of the rites of passage relating to the birth, membership of social institutions, marriage and death (Ringlon-Theilon).
9. Belief in the redemption and salvation of soul in heaven for good doers and retribution by the divine for bad doers.
10. Belief in the performance of festivals, ceremonies and rituals and other forms of religious and cultural expression of the worship of the divine.

These tenets clearly establish the Tingkao Ragwang Chapriak as a well formulated distinct religion with a well defined theological foundation.

The indigenous Zeliangrong religion has been christened with a distinct name; the nameless religion has become a name specific. The religion is regulated and managed by a supreme religious authority named the Zeliangrong Religious Council which has two important organs; the Executive Council and the Ecclesiastical Council.

The House of worship, named Kalum Kai was constructed. There are prayer cum religious congregation on every full moon day and every sunday both at the central place of worship and at the villages and individual families.

The oral customs relating to the rites of passage have been written and published in the form of scripture: Ringlon-Theilon, prayer-hymns have been composed and published. Songs and hymns in cassettes have been produced and distributed.

Symbol (Boudaan)

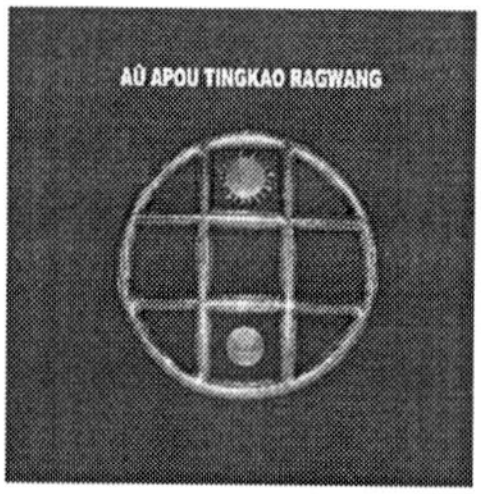

The council adopted the above as the symbol (Boudaan) of Tingkao Ragwang.

1. The circle represents the universe/cosmos
2. Criss-cross lines within the circle represent the Zodiac in the sky
3. The sun and the moon represent the heavenly bodies which are the creation of Tingkao Ragwang.

(The symbol is now widely used for all religious purposes. It is originally based on the circle used in the ceremony of Tingkao Ragwang Jaang Lamei)

The concept of Tingkao Ragwang, the heavenly God and Supreme God

The Tingkao Ragwang Chapriak is basically based on the fundamental belief on the Supreme God, Tingkao Ragwang. Tingkao Ragwang literally means the Heavenly God, or God of the sky or Lord of the universe. He is worshipped as the Supreme God, the creator of the universe, nature, gods, men and animals. Tingkao Ragwang according to Zeliangrong tradition, hymns and rites is endowed with all the divine elements ascribed to God.

i. Tingkao Ragwang is eternal; no beginning and no end
ii. Tingkao Ragwang is the creator of the universe
iii. Tingkao Ragwang is good and benevolent
iv. Tingkao Ragwang is the source of life, giver of the soul and the ultimate goal of the human soul
v. Tingkao Ragwang is the architect of men's destiny
vi. Tingkao Ragwang is the source of knowledge and wisdom
vii. Tingkao Ragwang is described and known by different names expressing the infinite versatile power of the divine. He is called Tingkao Ragwang, thw heavenly God.
    - Shamting Phianmei, one who plaits His hair (as men chant His name the plaited hair will fall apart)
    - Tingwang, God of Heaven or Sky
    - Somprai Gwang, King of gods worshipped by men (Somprai Gwang means creator of the uncreated and the destroyer of the created)
    - Pashumeipu Padammeipu, the creator of men
    - Tamshumeipu Tamjanmeipu, the ordainer of the need of human kind
    - Tingpuk Kandi Kasemmeipu, maker of the sky and earth
    - Kachak Dandi Pannumeipu, wearer of gold and silver
    - Bu-Nei Dammeipu, creator of the sun and moon
    - Bushinmeipu Buchameipu, giver and protector of soul
    - Himdaimeipu, weilder of power, the Almighty

These traditional appellates of Tingkao Ragwang show that Tingkao Ragwang is eternal. He has no beginning, no end. He is not created. He creates out of nothing by His will. He has no father, no mother. He just exists. He is benevolent, dispenser of welfare and prosperity to men. He is the creator of soul and the ultimate God of the soul.

He is really omniscient, omnipresent and omnipotent. Tingkao Ragwang is beyond time and space. What St. Anselm said about the timelessness and eternity of God in general is applicable to Tingkao Ragwang.

God exists neither yesterday, nor today, nor tomorrow but is absolutely outside all time. For yesterday, today and tomorrow are completely in time; however though nothing can be without God. God is nevertheless not in place or time but all things are in God. For nothing contains God but God contains all things.

The abode of Tingkao Ragwang is in the Tingkao Kaidai or Heaven or Tingkao Ragwang Kai. Tingkao Ragwang is omnipresent.

Creation: Universe, Gods and Men

According to the myths and traditions, Tingkao Ragwang willed to create the universe, gods, men and nature. He first created two primeval god and goddess, Didimpu and Didimpui (or Sudimpu and Sudimpui). As per will of Tingkao Ragwang, they created the sun, the moon, the stars, the water, the wind, the fire, the earth and seven layers of the earth, the seven layers of water and seven layers of the sky... And God created men.

The concept of soul

What is soul? Soul is the immortal spiritual element of human person. Soul is the essence or animating element of individual life. The soul resides in the human body. So long it resides in the human person, the man is alive. The moment it leaves the body permanently, the man dies. Presence or absence of a soul is the indicator of the life or death of a person. Soul is ordained by God. He is the source of soul and life. It is Tingkao Ragwang who gives soul to man…Soul has no body. Soul is not mundane and not material. Soul is the heart of an entity, the human person…Soul emanates from Tingkao Ragwang. And the goal of a soul is Tingkao Ragwang Himself.

Heaven, the abode of Tingkao Ragwang

The Tingkao Ragwang Chapriak believes in the existence of heaven known as Tingkao Kaidai or Tingkao Ragwang Kandi, the abode of Tingkao Ragwang. It is believed that the heaven is in the sky…Everything is available in heaven. There is no suffering, no pain, no unhappiness, no hunger, no worry, no jealousy and no anger in heaven. It is a golden land of peace and happiness. A soul who will enter heaven is the one who is free from any sin (Non) blemish, he who is a doer of good in human life and follows the tenet of Tingkao Ragwang Chapriak.

The life after death: Taroiram, land of the dead

The Tingkao Ragwang Chapriak believes in the concept of life after death and the land of the dead, Taroiram. The human soul after the physical death will go to the land of the dead. He will lead another life in the world of the dead… According to Tingkao Ragwang Chapriak, death is not an end of human soul. It is a stage in the continous existence of soul. Dead is a change of the way of life of the soul. The death, rites and ceremonies are to ensure the safe and joyful journey of the soul to the land of the dead where the souls of its ancestors are leading a life of themselves.

Rebirth

The Tingkao Ragwang Chapriak believes in the permanency of the human soul. The soul is born and reborn in different forms of life; human, animal and plants...The concept of rebirth is based on the belief that doers of good or doers of bad will get divine salvation or retribution. Human life is depended on his action. The holy, uplifted and blessed soul of a person who is righteous and who performs his moral and spiritual duties towards Tingkao Ragwang, men and community will go to heaven. Once he goes to heaven he will not be reborn. And those who have committed unpardonable wrongs will go to the land of Thuntadijang and he will not be reborn.

Concept of sin

Sin is a deviation from or violation of the accepted spiritual, social and moral norms of a society. In Tingkao Ragwang Chapriak sin is known as "Non" which is committed when a man violates the social and moral code of conduct. It is believed that a man who commits the sin of both man and god is punished by both God and society. The divine punishment is in the form of death and transformation of his soul into lower forms of life like animals, insects and plants.

Mode of Worship

The Tingkao Ragwang Chapriak is a well formulated worship of the Supreme God, other gods of the earth, deities of villages and dead ancestors.

Neihmei: Neihmei is spiritual form of worship and prayer of the community and individuals to Tingkao Ragwang by abstaining from any work in the village...Neihmei is a collective form of worship of Tingkao Ragwang by the whole village community or individual families on the occasion of various agricultural operations or natural disasters. Neihmei is observed for the granting of plentiful harvest: It is also observed to ward off any danger from natural calamities due to earthquake, hailstorm, fire, attack by pests, insects and rodents...Neihmei is in short a prayer to Tingkao Ragwang.

The second mode of worship is called Ra Kalummei, prayer and worship of Supreme God...The third mode is Ra-Khaangmei which means propitiation to deities and lower deities not to disturb the human kind.

There is a worship of Tingkao Ragwang through different kinds of ceremonies and sacrifices...There is also a worship of seven brother gods...The worship of village deities and ancestor worship...On every ceremony or rite, the holy wine is offer to the following deities. (i) Tingkao Ragwang, (ii) Ditingmei, the god of the earth, Banglagwang known earlier as Didimpu, (iii) Kaipi Bambu, upper village deity, (iv) Kaiba Bambu, lower village deity, (v) Kairao, the ancestor, (vi) Propitiation of wine to para, an evil spirit.

Festivals: Cultural expression of the worship of Tingkao Ragwang

Culture and religion are inseparable in Tingkao Ragwang Chapriak. Culture is a vehicle of religion. Culture is a form of worship of God. The festivals performed by the Zeliangrong people through the ages are the cultural and aesthetic expressions of the worship of the divine. During the festivals people worship and pray to Him for welfare of men and bountiful harvests. The festivals are performed at the various stages of the agricultural operations according to the lunar calendar. There are no uniform dates for the performance and observation of the festivals. The festivals are the rejoicing of the community with prayer to Tingkao Ragwang for his blessings for plenty and welfare. The social and cultural values, the aesthetic and creativity are expressed through dance, songs and music. The festivals are both social and religious occasions. The Tingkao Ragwang Chapriak is sustained by the colourful festivals. The ritual dances, songs and Ho-Hoing invoking the Almighty are the forms of worship.

Apart from the tract on concept of Zeliangrong primordial religion, the religious Council of the Tingkao Ragwang Chapriak Phom published two books namely, The Philosophical Concept of Tingkao Ragwang Chapriak and Socio-Cultural and Spiritual Traditions of Zeliangrongs in 2011. The two books were edited by Chaoba Kamson, General Secretary of the religious council. The second one was published by Heritage Foundation Guwahati, Assam. The philosophical concept consists of commentaries on concept of Supreme God, concept of soul, theory of salvation, life after of death, concept of hell, concept of heaven, concept of sin and rebirth. It also deals with the role of priest and priesthood and the performance of festivals. Some of the comments made by Chaoba Kamson are of great interest. To a question put by a theology scholar of Chennai, who is Tingkao Ragwang? Chaoba replied, "Man is created by an invisible God. This invisible God is worshipped by the followers of Tingkao Ragwang Chapriak (TRC) since ancient times. When the follower of TRC dies, his soul goes to the abode of invisible God. This invisible God is none other than Tingkao Ragwang. Tingkao Ragwang is the Supreme God. He is the creator of universe, nature, gods, man, animal, inanimate objects etc. He is really omnipresent, omnipotent, omniscient and omnibenovolent".

To a question, is Tingkao Ragwang created as a being or not? Chaoba Kamson replied, "Tingkao Ragwang always exists and is created by none. He creates natural objects like fire, wind, water, light, celestial body etc. He is eternal, no beginning and no end". He continued that when nothing existed Tingkao Ragwang already existed. Everything originated from Him. As to the question, how Tingkao Ragwang is visible? He said, "Tingkao Ragwang has no definite shape or form. He may be in the form of...as desire by Him. Therefore Tingkao Ragwang is invisible. He further said that though invisible by man, it is believed that the existence of Tingkao Ragwang through learning of history on theology, folklore, revelation of diviner, priest, priestess and performance of religious practices and hymns. He also stated that Tingkao Ragwang is the male God who has no wife, no parents, no brother and no sister. All living beings are His children. Chaoba's responses on the concept of sin, hell, land of the dead are of great interest. To a question on the construction of temple, Chaoba replied that there is no temple culture before the advent of Haipou Jadonang. Worship of Tingkao Ragwang in the temple was first introduced by Haipou Jadonang. Haipou Jadonang constructed temple named Kaokai at the villages of Kambiron, Nungkoa, Kekru and Binakandi in Assam.

The Socio-Cultural and Spiritual Traditions of Zeliangrong consists of four important write ups. The first one deals with Heraka: the primordial religion of Zeliangrong written by Pautanzan Newme. The second deals with the concept of soul in Tingkao Ragwang Chapriak by Chaoba Kamson. The third is Gods and goddesses of the Zeliangrong community written by Lanbilung Gonmei and the fourth is the funeral rites of the Zeliangrong people by Dr. Budha Kamei. Newme deals with the basic features of Heraka religion and its culture, genesis and the philosophy of Heraka religion, the concept of God, mode of worship, Munseniu ki (Holy Bhuban Cave), Heraka Kelum Ki (Heraka temple), the role of Peiki and Heraka festivals. Newme's paper deals with both social institution and religious organization of the Heraka. Chaoba Kamson's paper on the concept of soul in Tingkao Ragwang Chapriak deals with the source of soul, definition of soul and concept of heaven known as Tingkao Kaidai or Kandi. He also explains the concept of land of the dead known as Taroiram and rebirth, sin and hell in the Tingkao Ragwang Chapriak. His commentary is fresh and draws the reader's attention. Lanbilung Gonmei's paper describes the nature of Tingkao Ragwang, the worship of seven brother gods of Ragwang which are worshipped by Zeliangrong people. They are Ragwang, god of the lower realm, Bisnu, which is known by different names Munseniu, Manchanu, Bonchanu, Chonchai, Naapsinmei, Charakilongmei, Koklou and Karangong. He refers to several deities known as Shong and Bambu worshipped in the villages. He also refers to Purumkhang and Purumlu, the deities of the adolescents which are to be propitiated by appropriate ritual. Dampapu and Dampapui, deities at birth, Kambuipui and Charaipei, the goddess of grain and wealth and the ancestor worship performed by every household. Lanbilung thinks that the gods and goddesses and their mode of worship make the survival of Zeliangrong community against proselytization by the alien religions. He wrote, 'development of literatures on spiritual and philosophical aspects of a community will inspire the devotees who are in a state of transition from primitive to modernization and globalization. Literatures play a vital role'. Dr. Budha Kamei's Funeral rites of the Zeliangrong people is a well written and well documented research paper dealing with death and dead ceremonies. The concept of the land of the dead and the dead ceremonies performed during the funeral has been well explained. He says, "Theimei meaning death is a Zeliangrong word. Death is the last event of a life cycle of an individual. Death signifies the total cessation of life's process that eventually happens in all beings. The usual theory of process of death is a separation of the soul from the body". Dr. Budha describes the details of the funeral ceremony from the moment a person dies to the burial of the death. He again observes, "Funerary rites do not usually terminate with the disposal of the corpse by burial. Post funerary ceremonies and customs generally have two, not necessarily mutually exclusive motives to purify the mourners and to mourn the dead. When the funeral is ended, all who have taken part in the funeral must commonly be purified. Purification means the ritual which is used to protect against unclean, sinful and undesirable situations". Dr. Budha's paper is very illuminating observation on the funeral rites of the Zeliangrong people.

The formation of the Zeliangrong Religious Council in April 1994 was a land mark in the history of Zeliangrong people following the indigenous faith. The organizational leadership was provided by mature scholarly and highly committed intellectuals of Zeliangrong community. The people elected scholarly respectable gentleman named Prof. Mangthoi Thaimei to be the President of the Religious Council. The Council was organized in a democratic way. The three states of Manipur, Nagaland and Assam were represented in the Council. It appointed middle aged intellectuals mostly government employees to take up the organizational work. We may mention the role of Marulung Remei, a retired Joint Secretary of Manipur Secretariat Service who gave great intellectual support to the organization. The Council appointed three capable secretaries namely, Chaoba Kamson, Leirenjao Meiringmei and Lanbilung Gonmei who provided steel frame of the Council's organization. There was a popular support from the women folk of the community who had built up a great experience of pilgrimage to Bhuvan cave, the abode of Lord Bisnu. The pioneers of the youth wing were Makulim Remei who was the President of the Chabon Phom. Among the women leaders who provided a strong support to the organization were members of the Zeliangrong Women Fellowship (Mathenmei Phom) who were active in their respective villages. In the beginning the village elders gave active support to the organization. There was massive financial donation coming towards the Council. The Council constructed a House of Worship of Tingkao Ragwang named Kalum Kai at north Imphal in the village of Chingmeirong. The Council constructed a massive house of worship which attracted attention of the people both Zeliangrong and non Zeliangrong of all religious denomination. Many donated to the cause of the construction of the house of worship. Employees of the government numbering about 300 donated money every month to run the organization. The Zeliangrong Religious Council attracted support, sympathy and cooperation from several religious organizations. Of the social welfare organization, the Akhil Bharatiya Vana Vasi Kalyan Ashram extended both financial and intellectual support. The Council sponsored the construction of several house of worship (Kalum Kai) in Manipur both in the hills and plains. So far nearly 20 house of worship had been constructed with people's contribution.

The Zeliangrong Religious Council from the very beginning took up many important publication works in the form of souvenirs published on important occasions dealing with the philosophy of their religion. They published several editions of religious hymns and prayers to be used in the religious congregation in the house of worship or on important places. They published a scripture known as Ringlon-Theilon and many religious tracts both in English and Rongmei dialects. The Kalum Kai at the Rongmei village of Chingmeirong had become a landmark of Imphal city and a large number of visitors both from India and abroad visited the house of worship. Another cultural achievement of the organization was the declaration of Gaan Ngai festival as a state holiday in Manipur state. The Government of Assam made this festival as restricted holiday. The Zeliangrong people who follow the indigenous religion which has been named as Tingkao Ragwang Chapriak (TRC) has won a place of respect, honour and dignity among the tribal people of north east India.

The philosophy of Heraka

Rani Gaidinliu stated that during the last pilgrimage of Haipou Jadonang and herself to the holy cave of Bhuvan which is believed to be the abode of Lord Bisnu, Tingkao Ragwang the Supreme God also popularly known as Tingwang revealed His teachings. After Jadonang's death in August, 1931 a young Gaidinliu took up the leadership of the Zeliangrong revolt. The British arrested her and imprisoned her for life. She was released at the time of India's independence from Tura Jail. She was not allowed to enter her native state of Manipur for five years and she was settled among the Chang people at the village of Yimrap in Mon district of present Nagaland. She returned to Manipur and led a peaceful life by devoting herself in development activities of her people under the guidance of Prime Minister Pandit Jawaharlal Nehru. This period coincided with the Naga insurgency under the leadership of A.Z. Phizo. There grew up two basic differences between her and the Naga rebels. Rani Gaidinliu was a nationalist and opposed the Naga separatist movement. She also stood for the preservation of her religion, culture and way of life which were not wanted by the Naga rebels who were for the spread of Christianity. She went underground for six years to fight for her ideals: Indian nationalism and protection of her religion. In 1966, she came overground and led a peaceful life. Rani Gaidinliu found that most of her followers who came overground joined the Nagaland armed police. At the same time several Christian missionaries had converted her followers into Christian faith particularly Catholic Christianity. Therefore Rani Gaidinliu with her intimate social networking organized her religion and named 'Zeliangrong Heraka Association'. She gave a name to the religion which the Supreme God, Tingwang revealed to her master Haipou Jadonang and herself in the holy cave of Bhuvan in January 1931. Naming of her faith by Rani Gaidinliu was her response to the insinuating criticism of her religion by her Christian opponents who described her group as Kampai or Araka which means disorganized people. Personality of Rani Gaidinliu attracted the attention of all people and she appointed late N.C. Zeliang, a former Christian theologian, a government official, a political leader and a great singer to be the President of the Zeliangrong Heraka Association. Under his dynamic leadership, Heraka cult became popular in Zeliangrong areas and in most parts of tribal India. Rani Gaidinliu continued to be the patron-saint of the Heraka cult. After the death of N.C. Zeliang, the leadership of Zeliangrong Heraka Association was taken up by two committed leaders. One is Ramkuiwangbe Newme who was elected the President of the Zeliangrong Heraka Association of North East India. Ramkuiwangbe Newme is a very rich landowner in Haflong and retired official of Education Department of Assam. He became a preceptor and the priest of Heraka cult. With his wide influence, Heraka Association was well organized. He involved several educated Zeliangrong youth in this religious movement. The second is Pautanzan Newme who was elected the General Secretary of the Association. Under the leadership of these two leaders, Zeliangrong Heraka Assaociation organized their organizational branches in Zeliangrong villages of Assam, Nagaland and some parts of Manipur. They organized regular conferences in which teachings of Rani Gaidinliu and Heraka are well spread. The Zeliangrong Heraka Association was helped by the Visva Hindu Parishad in Assam and a Nagaland Vikash Parishad in the state of Nagaland. The Association published several hymns and religious texts.

They published the Herakame Leu which contains 503 hymns and prayers. Pautanzan Newme is a scholar in his own right. He wrote several religious texts in English which are published by the Association. The publications are Zeliangrong Customary Laws (in English), 2009 and Heraka: the primordial religion and its revitalization movement, 2011. He also wrote another tract on Heraka: the primordial religion of Zeliangrong in 2011 in a book entitled, Socio-Cultural and Spiritual Traditions of Zeliangrongs published by Heritage Foundation, Guwahati. These three publications of Pautanzan Newme gave an intellectual expression on the philosophy of Heraka religion. In this chapter it is proposed to deal with the Heraka concept of God, their mode of worship, temple culture (Kelum Ki) and other functionaries of Heraka religion including songs and dances, birth ceremony, dead rituals, rebirth, heaven and land of the dead. Pautanzan writes on the concept of God, "Zeliangrong people believe in the existence of one Supreme God known as Tingwang who is the creator of the universe, the sun and the moon and all living beings. He is omnipresent, omnipotent, omniscient and all benevolent. With the direction of Tingwang, Heraka religion was first introduced by the great God Banglagwang for the mankind of all corners. Thus Heraka religion is not a man made. Heraka literally means 'Pure' or 'not impure' which was spelled out by the Supreme God...Heraka is the religion which was revealed by Tingwang to Gaidinliu in her last pilgrimage to Bhuvan cave – said Gaidinliu. Thus the main concept of Heraka religion is that those, whosoever could obey the authentic principles of Heraka religion would be blessed good fortune in their life and also the immortal souls of good doers would go to the abode of Tingwang. So, we the Heraka people believe in Him only" (Newme, 2011,p 26, Guwahati). The Heraka had devised a well regulated mode of worship which is dependent on devotion and worship to

Supreme God. They worship on every full moon day at the House of Prayer (Kelum Ki). They have adopted 10 rules of worship and prayer to God.

1. Gathering at Kelumki early in the morning
2. Recites hymns and offer collective sunrise prayer
3. The priest offer prayer to Almighty god
4. Entering into Kelumki singing devotional song
5. Individual prayer at the holy Altar
6. Sing a benedictory song
7. Announcement and time given to speak on Heraka Hingde
8. Singing a rejoicing song in praise of God
9. Exultant prayer by the priest upon the offertories
10. Taking a Telau dui (Holy water).

Heraka has adopted the temple culture (Heraka Kelumki). Heraka believes in the worship of God in Kelumki (house of worship). A construction of temple was started by Haipou Jadonang and the architecture of Kelumki or God's House was revealed to Haipou Jadonang. The Heraka Kelumki is believed to be the second holiest place besides the Holy Bhuvan cave. Those who could not go to Bhuvan cave may offer prayer to Tingwang at Kelumki. Heraka religion is organized through the office of the Heraka Tingkupau, the priest who is a head of the village. He plays a leading role in all religious activities of the village. The eldest male member who have enough courage and experience in worship and control his villagers is selected as the Tingkupau.

Paiki is a sanctum of Heraka which is honoured by all Heraka followers. Paiki is selected from among the individual houses in every village. A person who is devoted to Tingwang may be honoured with the running of the Paiki. The head of the Paiki is called Paipeu or Paipui.

Heraka has elaborate burial rituals. They also believed in the rebirth of the human soul. While the human being dies the soul is not dead. Herakas believe that there is a kingdom of God in heaven which is known as Tingimram (heaven) and land of the dead known as Heruimeram. There is a strong believe that man's soul would go to heaven or land of the dead.

Heraka believed in the directives and inspirations revealed by Rani Gaidinliu. Pautanzan writes, "Again Rani Gaidinliu was inspired and taught by the Almighty God in her trances dream that offering of animals, sacrificial worship to God (Tingwang) is not required as such offering is not accepted by Him but those were eaten by the demons (evil spirits). In view of the fact that Gaidinliu tried her best to teach her people the primordial Heraka religion in four phases". After 30 years of preaching Rani Gaidinliu declared in a public meeting on 11th day of January 1990 at Kipeilo village in Assam that the sacrificial worship to God is not needed. Therefore sacrifices of animals are to be totally avoided or abolished. One can perform prayer with a clean mind and body at any specific time and day by reciting the holy psalms and sing the devotional songs freely (Newme, Heraka the primordial religion.. p.34). The holy prayer chanted by Heraka follower at the time of worship is again reproduced by Pautanzan Newme, "Heh, thou art the King of the universe and heaven, the human beings. The creator of earth and heavenly bodies, the sun and the moon, all the creature and living things. Administering the spiritual souls of mankind. The giver of all boons and complete reign over all corners of earth and heaven". He also quoted Rani Gaidinliu who said, "Whenever you suffer from ailments or miseries - pray to God for the longevity of the sick man's life and to heal the suffering through His grace in your prayer".

Every prayer concludes with the following incantation. O Lord Tingwang, with the above circumstances described are prayed for to shower your blessings and to absolve from all inadvertent words in my prayer. O Lord Tingwang, Kelum. (Newme p. 35)

Impact of Christianity

Conversion of the Zeliangrong people was started in early 20th century; it had a small beginning. The first Zeme convert of the Naga Hills district of Assam was baptized on 31st December 1905 and then two persons of Benreu village namely, Kanese and Ensarangba were baptized in 1910 and the first Baptist Church was established in this village. The first Zeme of North Cachar Hills (Dima Hasao) was one Dituting Npame of Kenararam village and the first church was established in this village. In Manipur, the first Rongmei convert was Maipak who was baptized by Rev U.M. Fox at Imphal on 5th December, 1915. Maipak or Namrijinang and Kachindai were Zeliangrong converts based at Keishamthong Rongmei village of Imphal. The church historian, Mp. Namthiurei gives a life history of Maipak.

"Maipak was born in Khaukin village in Tamenglong. His mother died young and son he was brought up by his father. An epidemic occurred in the village and the villagers shifted to Aling. Later his family came down to Imphal and settled at Keishamthong in search of livelihood...The Maharaja (of Manipur) recruited him to the Manipur State Police and he became a palace guard. Maipak was quite talented and joined the Maharaja's band. The Maharaja was impressed by his music and he was ultimately appointed the band master of the Maharaja's police. And he lived at Keishamthong which was a colony of the employees of the Manipur State Police, Band party and Palace guards...He converse with two evangelists, Teba Karong and Longkhovel and studied the Bible in Manipuri. In 1914 he and his wife embraced Christianity. The family was blessed with a son named David Kaphunlung, 'seed of life'...Maipak ...was baptized at Imphal creating a furore between the Manipur State Durbar and the Mission. Maipak and his friends built a small thatched hut at Keishamthong village for worship. This was called the Church. Rev. Pettigrew used to visit the Church and meet the new converts. The villagers of Keishamthong were not happy with the conversion of Maipak and his Christian activities" (Mp. Namthiurei, The Great Awakening, 1972).

Starting from such a small beginning, Christian missionary activities in Zeliangrong area were taken up by indigenous Christian leadership. With the appointment of K. David, Keithonang and Dinthuiyeng as the superintending pastor of the north west association which cover Tamenglong sub division. In 1949, Zeliangrong Christian Association was opened at the village of Khongjaron. Among the foreign missionaries, two sympathizers were an American lady named, Miss Julia A. Rose (1905 -1994) and Rev. J.S. Anderson gave great help. Historian Gangmumei Kamei observed, "Rev. Anderson and Miss Rose were two great friends and sympathisers of the Zeliangrong people". The American Baptist Mission was followed by the Catholic mission and Seven Day Adventist.

Christianity had brought about education in early period with their mission primary schools when the conservative Zeliangrong people refused to attend the government schools. With frequent contacts between the Christian followers and foreign missionaries, their world view and mindset had been broadened. The Zeliangrong Christian accepted modernity with economic development. If one looks into Christian missionary activities in Zeliangrong area, there was no much help from the foreign missionaries. The Christian missionary movement was more or less an indigenous effort. Unfortunately the Christian missionaries in their enthusiasm to spread Christianity, tried to destroy the indigenous social and cultural life. They prohibited the performance of Zeliangrong dance and music; they also prohibited the dormitory system and even encouraged the Christian villagers to defy the authority of the traditional village council. Christianity had done a great damage to the Zeliangrong culture. The followers of the indigenous Zeliangrong religion had withstood the onslaught of Christian evangelism that there could be education, improved standard of living, government employment, economic development and modernization even without conversion into Christianity. A philosophical reply to the Christianity is now provided by the Heraka cult with their belief in one Supreme God (Tingwang) and the Tingkao Ragwang Chapriak (TRC), the traditional religion of the Zeliangrong people.

Kalum Kai of Tingkao Ragwang Chapriak (TRC) of Imphal

Mass Prayer for longevity at Kalum Kai, Imphal

THE HERAKA

Symbol of Heraka

Symbol (Boudan) of Tingkao Ragwang

LEADERS OF THE TRC

R. Marulung, President TRC

Chaoba Kamson, General Secretary, TRC

Leirenjao Meiringmei, General Secretary, TRC

Lanbilung Gonmei, Executive Secretary, TRC

Kalum Ki of Heraka, Lodiram, Assam

Footprint of Rani Gaidinliu, Hangrum, Assam

Heraka devotees in front of Kalum Ki, Hangrum, Assam

Late N.C. Zeliangrong, First President of Zeliangrong Heraka Association

Ramkuiwangbe Newme, President, Zeliangrong Heraka Association, North East India

Pautanzan Newme, General Secretary, Zeliangrong Heraka Association, NE India

Chamkandai Kamei, social and religious leader of Zeliangrong (Silchar)

4

A People with a Rich Culture

The festivals of the Zeliangrong people are a cultural expression of their religious belief. Festivals are an aesthetic form of worship of God. Since the Zeliangrong people are an agrarian community, their festivals are performed in all seasons according to their agricultural calendar and every festival is associated with a stage of the agricultural operations in the year. The festivals are also associated with their religion, the worship of the Supreme God, Tingkao Ragwang or Tingwang with worship for success in cultivation and for bountiful harvest. The festivals are organized on the customary directives of the elders of the Village Council and they are performed through the dormitories of the youth of the village. The festivals are known as 'Ngi' or 'Ngai'. The Zeme and Liangmai term is 'Ngi' and the Rongmei term is 'Ngai'. It appears that Liangmai was a first social formation of the Zeliangrong people and since Liangmai term for a festival is 'Ngi' therefore it has been argued that the common term for the festivals performed by other cognate groups of the Zeliangrong people should be called 'Ngi'. The literal meaning of 'Ngi' or 'Ngai' means 'rejoicing'. There are local variations of the festivals among the three cognate groups.

According to traditions, the Zeliangrong people had developed a culture and civilization based on shifting agriculture when they arrived at Makuilongdi. A historian observes that, "Makuilongdi was the cradle of Zeliangrong culture. A well developed society based on shifting agriculture with polity which look like a chiefdom with influence over other villages established by brothers and sons of (Chief) Nguiba. They spoke a language akin to the Maram and Thangal. In the social formation, only the Liangmai language speakers formed the social and cultural entity. The language they spoke was perhaps Hana or Hamei, the original language of the Liangmai. At Makuilongdi the people was divided into two major clans, Pamei and Newmei...The exodus from Makuilongdi was caused by the pressure of land due to the increase in population, differences on the issue of succession to the hereditary chieftanship. There could not have been a sudden break up; but gradual migration of groups from Makuilongdi" (Gangmumei Kamei, A History of Zeliangrong Nagas). However according to tradition, Makuilongdi village had been highly populated and prosperous. There were 30 boys and girls dormitories; there were construction of 30 Taraang Kais and ceremonial houses. The people had forgotten the sense of time as the whole community was engaged in these ceremonies. A divine communication was given to the villagers that the year had ended and people were advised to resort to the agricultural activities. The people were frightened of the wrath of God and they fled and making a sudden exodus from Makuilongdi. A group went to north and became Zeme; a second group went south and became Rongmei and the original settlers who stayed back at Makuilongdi became the Liangmais, the northerner. It was at Makuilongdi that culture of the Zeliangrong people was fully developed. Religious beliefs and social customs were developed. The religion of the people based on worship of God through the great sacrifices and propitiation was developed. We can deduce that the festivals and religious ceremonies were developed by the Zeliangrong people while they were inhabited at Makuilongdi.

Several myths indicated that there were prophets and law givers who advised the people to follow customs and usages for the society. Tingpurengsonang who was a divine patriarch of the dormitory which was attended by deities, men and animals was the first prophet to give guidelines to man to live in society. Another law giver was Amangbow who performed a great ceremonial feast known as Amang Joulube while constructing a ceremonial house. Another law giver was Tenglaam who for the first time laid down the mode of worship of God. He according to the myth became a priest advisor of God known as Charamukhandijungpu (priest advisor of God). Thus worship of God, performance of festivals and ceremonies were historically developed.

The Liangmai group who lived at Makuilongdi was first people to develop the festivals which have been categorized as follows.

1. Nanu (ear boring festival of the children)
2. Maleng (Seed sowing completion festival)
3. Paropngi/Pokphatngi (festival of new crops)
4. Chakak Ngi (Soul departing festival)
5. Chaga Ngi/Gaan Ngi (winter festival)
6. Rih Ngi (Festival of war)

The Rongmeis also developed festivals more or less on the line of the Liangmai festivals. Rongmei festivals have become more elaborated reflecting the attitude towards social organization, agricultural development, maintenance of ponds and paths, seed sowing and towards religion and war. The following 10 festivals of the Rongmeis are indicative of the growing social philosophy of Rongmei people.

1. Nanu (ear boring festival of the children)
2. Napkaodai (Ginki) (Seed sowing festival)

3. Gudui (Maleng) (Completion of seed sowing cultivation festival)
4. Tun Ngai (Festival of rains to improve ponds, path and village street)
5. Ten Ngai (Festival of bun)
6. Puakphat Ngai (Fesival of new crops)
7. Donjao Ngai/Banchat Ngai (Declaration of the largest producer of paddy)
8. Chakak Ngai (Soul departing festival)
9. Gaan Ngai (Chaga) (Winter festival)
10. Rih Ngai (Festival of war)

The Zemes who were divided into two groups; the western Zeme who migrated towards west of the Barial Range and Barak river and the northern Zeme who migrated from Nui or Yang towards the north in the present south Nagaland. These two sections developed linguistic differentiation but more or less their society, religion and culture remain the same. The following are the festivals performed by Zeme section.

Name	*Season (Month)*	*Purpose*
1. Helei Kaneba (Ngi)	Kene/Kazeng (Feb-Mar)	Beginning of seed sowing
2. Nchang Ngi	Gepei (May)	Completion of seed sowing
3. Puakpat Ngi	Hechet (September)	Completion of cultivation
4. Nsim Ngi	Heru/Heba (fall season)	Beginning of the harvest festivals
5. Hega Ngi	Ndue (December)	Winter festival (Post harvest and soul departing festival)

Of these festivals, three festivals are of almost similar duration, same season and same purpose. They are the

Hega Ngi of the Zemes, Gin Ngi or Chaga Ngi (Gadi) of the Liangmais and the Gaan Ngai of the Rongmeis. Some festivals are described in the following paragraph.

Zeliangrong Heraka festivals

The Zemes have adopted Heraka cult and the festivals prescribed by the Heraka authorities are now performed in their respective villages. Since they use the term Zeliangrong Heraka in all their dealings, the Zeliangrong Heraka festival is adopted to mean the Zeme festivals. The following are the festivals performed by this group.

Helei Kaneba (Helei Ngi)

Helei Ngi literaly means festival observed before seed sowing in gardens and jhums. This festival is celebrated for three days in the month of February/March in the Zeme month of Kejing keu. It is a first festival of year. The Zeliangrong customary laws give a description of Helei Ngi as followed by the Heraka people.

i. Individual prayer at Kelumki at sunrise. No sunrise prayer is performed.

ii. Gathering at Paiki

iii. The priest offer prayer

iv. Singing of Mejaleu – three times

v. Enter into the Paiki while singing devotional songs

vi. Strictly observe festival in the following three days

a). Prayer day (Kakelumbe mai), b). Main festival day (Ngi di mai) and c). Closing day of festival (Ngi kam bemai)

According to Gangmumei Kamei, this festival marks the beginning of the agricultural process, after the preparation of the jhum filed. It is the seed sowing festival. Every household worships the Supreme God, Tingwang for the blessings of a plentiful harvest. The Tingkupeu, the priest observes fasting, genna is observed from the next day, and the seed sowing is started.

Nchang Ngi

This festival is observed to mark the completion of seed sowing in jhum fields. The priest performs sacrifice for good crops, protection from pests and damage by animals and for good harvest. The villagers observed genna the whole day. The festival is celebrated in the month of May (Gepeikeu) for three days. Usually animal sacrifice is offered during the festival. Now with the Heraka reforms, the offering of animal sacrifice is abolished.

This festival is observed to mark the completion of the cultivation of the early crops. The completion of the work (Kagenwanba) is declared by the village priest. Every household must complete the work before this day. A genna is observed in the village, no cutting of firewood and no husking of paddy. A pig or a fowl is sacrificed to Tingwang. And the pieces of the liver of the pig are distributed to every household. Sometimes even mithun is sacrificed to Tingwang. And the meat is distributed to every household, which observes genna and offers sacrifices to the Tingwang. This Nchang Ngi is equivalent to the Nap Kaodai (Ginki) of the Liangmai and Rongmei (Gangmumei Kamei, A History of the Zeliangrong Nagas From Makhel to Rani Gaidinliu, 2004, p. 305).

Puakpat Ngi

After the observance of Nchang Ngi, Puakpat Ngi is performed to mark the beginning of the harvesting season. This festival is observed in the month of Hebaikeu (September) in autumn season. Puakpat Ngi is the festival of getting new crops. The priest performs worship on Puakpat Ngi praying that the new harvest crops be inexhaustible even after extravagant consumption. The process of worship is similar to that of Helei Ngi. The festival is obsèrved at least for three days.

According to Gangmumei Kamei, this festival is performed to mark the beginning of the harvesting season.the ecrops are ripe and ready for harvesting. There is a period of some recess in the agricultural works. A mithun was sacrificed. Ans a mithun chase was organized for competitors among the youth. U.G. Bower writes, "It was autumn now and the first of the great harvest festivals had begun. The early rice was coming in the week of summer were over, village after village was celebrating the festival known as Puakage (Puakpat)". She described the mithun chase at Laisong village as very exciting, adventurous and dangerous. The wome do not sleep with their husbands. Men also do not eat rice and beef. They drink rice beer and other meats. Genna is observed on the second day and the harvesting starts from the third. Every household offers a fowl to Tingwang and shares the meat. Puakpat Ngi is performed as Puakphat by the Liangmai and the Rongmei.

Nsim Ngi

The Nsim Ngi is the festival of the youth of the village which is celebrated in the month of Kerukeu (November). This is a merry making festival. All young boys and girls rejoice during the festival wearing beautiful traditional attires. They serve drinks and meals freely as it is the festival of the youth. Singing and dancing are compulsory during the festival. No prayer or worship by the priest is required. The festival is sometimes converted to Hangleu Ngi or Metui Ngi. This festival is celebrated when the village yields more wealth and good health of the villagers. As such most of the Zeliangrong villages do not celebrate this Nsim Ngi at present.

Hepumra Teube (Festival of New Year)

Zeliangrong Heraka people observed Hepumra (New Year Day) on the new moon day just after 14-15 days of the observation of Hega Ngi festival (which is being described in the next chapter). The New Year Day is regarded as the purest and holiest day of the year. So the family members should be present at their respective homes to observe it. They strictly observed prohibition to do the household work, to travel, to cut firewood, to sell or buy anything, to pluck leaves, to wash clothes, to husk rice, to cut hair. Husbands are strictly forbidden to sleep with their wives for two days. The priest performs ritual worship on that day for the longevity, good health and prosperity of the whole village. (This information on the Heraka festivals was based on Zeliangrong Customary Laws published by Zeliangrong Heraka Association, 2009, Haflong). This was confirmed by Ramkuiwangbe Newme, President of the Zeliangrong Heraka Association who gave a verbal interview to the author which she recorded in her diary on 24th January, 2012 at Lodiram.

We found local variation in the performance of festivals among the Zeme section of the Zeliangrong. Kuije Disong, a 65 year old elder of Katang village of Tamenglong district of Manipur gives the following festivals performed in his village.

1. Hemei maje lalei performed in the month of May to mark the completion of seed sowing. It is a one day festival in which the sisters of the householder are invited to a feast in her brother's house.

2. Hemeurache Ngi is performed in the month of August for five days. It is to mark harvest of new crops. Men folk collected firewood for consumption for one year for the boys' dormitory. In Katang village during this festival, the ceremony of Matui is performed.

3. Nsim Ngi is performed in the month of October for 11 days. During this festival, Hen Ngi which is a children

registration ceremony is performed. An occasion of the festival is called Kajepui sing puabe in which boys of the dormitory collected firewood for the female owner of the dormitory and the lady served feast for the boys. Tasim simle is also performed in which the dormitory boys repair paths and water ponds. They do feasting, drinking wine, and wrestling at the village gate. It is followed by a hohoing procession from the village gate to the dormitory. Next day the members of the dormitory bring eatables as gifts to the dormitory.

4. Hekak Ngi. In the village of Katang, Hekak Ngi is performed in the month of December. It is a very elaborate festival. The graveyard of the dead during the past one year is made. It is to give farewell to the dead and is known as Herau kathabe. Therefore it is also called Kachai Ngi, the festival of the dead.

Hekak Ngi is followed by Hega Ngi in January which is equivalent with the Chaga or Gaan Ngai of other cognate groups of other Zeliangrong people. This information was provided to the author by the informant in an interview held on 27th February 2012 at Imphal.

Keyidualieng Newme of Hejailo village of Dima Hasoa district of Assam provided the following information on the performance of Hekak Ngi before the adoption of the Heraka cult. According to him, Hekak Ngi is performed 4 days before Hega Ngi. It starts with a fasting before on the first day of the festival. Then the utensils and belongings of the dead are cleansed and it is followed by farewell feast in the afternoon. On the second day known as Heragua, a wild turmeric known as 'Ga' is collected from the forest for use in a ceremony to drive away the evil spirit. It is accompanied by a genna of the village. Next day is called Hegasau which is followed by Haga jaokai which is performed to prepare for the Hega festival. Hekak Ngi is performed prior to Hega Ngi. Hekak Ngi is the parting ceremony of the dead from the village. The villagers are engaged in the making of the graves, stone pulling ceremonies, erection of wooden poles and raising of stone slabs over the grave. Hekak Ngi is known as Chakak Ngi among the Liangmai and Chakak Ngai among the Rongmei before the Gaan Ngai festival.

Hekak Ngi

Though Hekak Ngi is performed as a part of the grat festival of Hega Ngi, it is of great relevance that we give a description of Hekak Ngi. As it has been noted earlier, Hekak Ngi is the parting ceremony of the souls of the dead from the village. During this festival, the villagers are engaged in the making of the graves, stone pulling ceremony, erection of wooden poles and raising of stone slabs over the graves. Miss Ursula Graham Bower, a British freelance anthropologist gives an eye witness account of the ceremony at Laisong village around 1942. She writes in her Naga Path (1950), "Hekak Ngi was the parting of the dead from the living. The Zemi believes in an after life. The dead, he thinks, live in their old homes until forced to go; and after a death in the house, and drinks are set out for the ghosts at every meal until ceremonial separation is complete. On feast days sometimes great bowls of pounded soap creeper (Khoi) thick with seed are put out so that the ghosts may bathe, like the living, and join the celebration. At Hekak Ngi comes the final parting. The last sacrifices are made. All that the dead will need in the next world, gourds, cloth, foods, seeds anything else omitted from the grave goods at burial must be provided now. When everything is done the priest goes up to the top of the village. Then when his ritual there is complete, he moves down the street, calling about, he bids the ghosts take their possession and go. When the last of the invisible ghosts has passed through the lower gateway and take the low road to the land of the dead, the old man shuts and returns again to a village implied of all but living men".

She continues, “The street was entirely deserted. Not a child, not a dog, not a chicken was out, a few men stood concealed in house porches, well behind the wood stacks; and the whole, long story, space was dear under the noon sun”.

“The priest had finished their ceremony at the upper gate, and was coming down. The old priest came into sight at the head of the street. There was not a breath of air. The old man’s hair glinted in the sunshine. His voice was unexpectedly clear in the hush. “O all you dead. Go to your own place and leave the living here. O!, all you dead, it is time to part. Let the living remain and let the dead go”.

“There was something indescribably melancholy in the cry. There was something eerie. It felt cold in spite of the windlessness and the sun. The old man passed on and he has now come back behind it”.

“Still nobody stirred. The silence lasted; perhaps for five or six minutes, and then we heard the priest’s voice proclamming as he returned”.

“The dead have gone to their own place. The dead are separated from the living. The dead have gone to their own place”.

After the Hekak Ngi was over, the village priests and the elders perform a rite of driving away of the evil spirits from the village. This is called Heragnabe. The priest offers a sacrifice of a dog with ginger and wild turmeric. The head of the dog with the jaws open by a bamboo piece was kept at the village to drie away the evil spirits. The Rongmeis call this as Rathaomei or Shimuntungmei.

The author also interviewed the Zeme elders of Kipeujang village of Peren district, Nagaland namely, Hingchube H. Zeliang, Vice President of Zeliangrong Heraka Association, Nagaland endorsed the following information of the festival performed by Zeliangrong heraka people. He mentioned that in Peren area, the Zemes performed Henajou which is a ceremony to celebrate the birth of children within one year.

The Liangmai Festivals

According to the Zeliangrong tradition, the Liangmai section evolved a well regulated culture expressed through their respective festivals performed during the different stages of the jhum cultivation. It is true that from amongst the Liangmais, Zeliangrong festivals, ceremonies, rites and rituals were eveloved. Even now, the Rongmeis are still using the archaic Liangmai language in their religious hymns and songs. The following festivals were evolved by the Liangmai sections who were the custodians of the Zelaingrong culture of Makuilongdi.

Nanu

This is called an ear boring festival. The children who were born in the prvious year are reported to the office of the Kengjapui (old women). The parents of the children bring eatables like vegetables, roots, fishes and salt cakes to the old women. The elders of the village performed Nanumei ceremony by offering sacrifices to Supreme God. The children who are born in the previous year are brought to the office of the Kengjapui and their ears were bored and given earrings made of lead or copper. The gifts of the children were distributed to the male and female elders of the village. In the afternoon the old women go around the houses of the parents of the children and sing the fertility songs. The youth before puberty also participate in this fertility procession known as Turamroi. This festival is performed for three days. This is followed by the Rongmei sections. The Nanu of the Liangmai and Rongmei are similar. This is performed in the month of February-March.

Maleng

The next festival performed is called Maleng. It is a seed sowing completion festival perfomed in the month of May.

Every household offers a fowl to God, Tingwang for giving good cultivation and good harvest.

Parop Ngi/ Puakphat Ngi

The coming of the new crops is celebrated with the performance of Puakphat Ngi or Parop Ngi. This is called the festival of new crops. With the coming of new harvest, the villagers gather new crops and when their granaries are full, they performed this festival, worshipping God and enjoying the recreation with feasting. This original festival of the Liangmais is performed both by the Zeme and Rongmei.

Chakak Ngi

The parting of the soul dead man from amongst the living is performed in the Chakak Ngi. This is performed among the Zemes as Hekak Ngi and among the Rongmeis, it is called Chakak Ngai. This is the festival of the departure of the dead from the life of the living. It is a very elaborate festival starting from the making of the graves of the dead, production of new fire, performance of ho hoing procession, indulging in competition for physical strengths like long jump and wrestling. It is concluded by a ritual asking the ghost of the dead to leave the village and driving away the evil spirits. This is called Raremmei and Shimuntungmei. We have given a description of Hekak Ngi as performed among the Zemes as recorded by Ursula Graham Bower. This is more or less similar with that of the Liangmais and the Rongmeis.

After the Chakak Ngi the next festival is Chaga Ngi which has been nowadays called Chaga Gadi. We will describe this Chaga Ngi in the next chapter.

Rih Ngi (War festival)

The Rih Ngi is performed after Chaga Ngi. It is performed to strengthen the military might of the village by performance of several rituals. Chong phenmei is a ritual in order to indicate the future of the village. An effigy made of plaintain tree or soft wood is put up and sharpen bamboo reeds in form of spear are thrown at the effigy to know the omen of good harvest, good hunting or successful raids against the enemy.

There develop variations in the Liangmai festival. K.D. Pamei, former Joint Director of Education, Government of Manipur who belongs to the village of Pabram village of Tamenglong district, Manipur gives the following festivals of his village. The villagers who were converted into Christianity have ceased to perform the festival. This is a reminiscence of his childhood days at his native place. He mentions the following festivals.

1. Bente Khaibon performed in February/march
2. Lupio Ngi: seed sowing performed in the month of March/April
3. Lumoa Ngi: festival of weeding in the month of May
4. Maruop performed in June/July during the flowering of crops
5. Kasan Ngi in July/August (new harvest)
6. Raogen Ngi in the month of September. It coincide with Puakphat Ngi
7. Chaga Ngi in the month of October
8. Tatui Ngi performed when there is good harvest in the village
9. Chakeik Ngi (Chakak Ngi)

The progress of Christian missionaries was complete; therefore the Liangmai Naga Baptist Council announced that there is no non Christian among the Liangmais. Therefore, Liangmai festivals ceased to exist among them. However this statement is not wholly true. There are several Liangmai persons who are highly educated and following their indigenous religion. There are doctors, officers and teachers who are leading the indigenous revitalization movement known as Zeliangrong Heraka Association. Mention may be made of Late N.C. Zeliang who was the President of the Zeliangrong Heraka Association, Dr. Wilubo Chawang of Dimapur, Puatanzan Newme, General Secretary of the Zeliangrong Heraka Association (Lodiram) and Ms. Tasile N. Zeliang, an educationist and writer of Nzau village of Peren district, Nagaland. These Liangmai leaders who lead the Heraka cult performed the following festivals.

1. Helei Ngi: This festival is a preparatory to the seed sowing.
2. Nchang Ngi: This festival is performed after the completion of seed sowing
3. Puakpat Ngi: This festival is performed to mark the coming of the new harvest
4. Nsim Ngi: This is a youth festival.
5. Chaga Ngi (Chaga Gadi): Post harvest festival
6. Chapumra (Hepumra): The New Year festival performed on the new moon day at the end of Pous month (January).

As per information provided by Ms. Tasile N. Zeliang, Deralung Nren and Epelung Nring the interview with the author was recorded at Jalukie-B village of Peren District of Nagaland on 16th February 2012.

The Rongmei Festivals

The Rongmei festivals are the most articulate of the festivals performed by the Zeliangrong community. Zeliangrong scholars have written enormously on their festivals. There are also scholars who tried to present the festivals in harmonization of the various festivals of the community. The effort of Dr. Budha Kamei, a research scholar of History to give a comprehensive account of the Rongmei festivals in relation to that of Zeme and Liangmai is commendable. Dr. Budha Kamei in "Ritual festivals of Zeliangrong" published in Gaan Ngai by The State Level Gaan Ngai Celebration Committee, Manipur, 2012, Imphal writes, "There are no peoples without religion. The Zeliangrong people of North East India also follow a profound indigenous religion known as Tingkao Ragwang Chapriak. Tingkao Ragwang Chapriak is basically based on the fundamental belief of Tingkao Ragwang, the Supreme God. Tingkao Ragwang literally means the Heavenly God, or God of the sky or Lord of the universe. R. Brown has made a reference that the Zeliangrong people worship a Supreme Being who is the creator of all. Tingkao Ragwang Chapriak means the religion of Tingkao Ragwang. This profound religious tradition is preserved and practiced through oral traditions by the ancient Zeliangrong community for ages. The population of Tingkao Ragwang Chapriak in the three states of Assam, Manipur and Nagaland is 29,000 souls approximately. The aim of this article is to delve the festivals of Tingkao Ragwang Chapriak"...

Dr. Budha Kamei continues, "Ngi meaning festival is a Zeliangrong word. The Zeliangrong people celebrate their festivals in all seasons and almost every month of the agriculture calendar. Every festival is associated with the stage of agricultural operation. Their rejoicing of festivals expresses through prayer and thanksgiving to God for good harvest and future prosperity. The honour and farewell to the dead ancestors is also reflected in the festival. The social and cultural values, the aesthetic and creative sense, their love of beauty and colour are expressed in these festivals. Gangmumei Kamei, a renowned historian of India writes, 'Festivals are a vehicle of religion and the Zeliangrong religion is sustained by their colourful festivals accompanied by religious rites and prayers, dance and music and feating during different months of a year'. Dancing, singing, eating and drinking are the four main highlights of festivals among the Zeliangrongs. It is said that festivals bind a religious group into a unity that transcends family and local ties... Each of the festivals is a sweet gift of God which is practiced with true religious faiths which makes human being a superior race and dominant creatures".

The Rongmei speakers of the Zeliangrong community who are inhabited in the state of Assam, Manipur and Nagaland and settled in nearly 150 villages following indigenous religion of Tinkao Ragwang Chapriak (TRC) perform the following festivals. The Rongmei speakers are found in Cachar or Barak valley of Assam. There are two sections of the Rongmei who are found in the Tamenglong district of Manipur divided into upper Rongmei and lower Rongmei because of their settlement respectively in northern side and southern side of the Zeliangrong habitat. There is another group of the Rongmei speakers who are settle in Manipur valley popularly known as the plain Rongmeis who lived in the Imphal valley among the Meitei settlers. In Nagaland, there are 14 Rongmei villages of which 3 performed the indigenous festivals following their TRC cult. They are in the urban localities of Zeliangrong village and Ragailong village in Dimapur town and Naga Bazar locality of the Rongmeis in Kohima town.

The following are the festivals performed by the Rongmei speakers of Zeliangrong community of the three states.

i. Gaan Ngai: The greatest festival of the people.
ii. Rih Ngai: The war festival
iii. Nanu Ngai: Ear boring festival
iv. Napkao Ngai: Seed sowing festival
v. Ginki Ngai: Worship of goddess of paddy
vi. Maleng (Gudui) Ngai: Festival marking the completion of seed sowing
vii. Tun Ngai: The festival of the rains

viii. Ten Ngai: Festival of bun
ix. Puakphat Ngai: The new harvest festival
x. Dongjao Ngai: A feast celebrating plentiful granary
xi. Chakak Ngai: Parting of the dead

The next chapter will deal with the Gaan Ngai festival.

Rih Ngai

Rih Ngai means a festival of war. (Rih means war and Ngai means festival). It is the reminisecence of wars and raids during the head hunting days of the past. It is now a peaceful celebration of the ritual festival. It is performed in the month of February after the Gaan Ngai festival. In some villages, mostly in the western basin of the Barak this festival is sometimes known as Chaga Ngai. On the eve of the festival every male of the boys' dormitory (Khangchu) observes fasting (Lumthengmei) for the purification of body, soul and mind of the male awrriors of the village. On this day there is a segregation between male and female; men do not touch women and do not eat or drink any food or water prepared by women. Therefore men folk cook separately. In the boys' dormitory, a pig is sacrificed and a portion of the pork is given to the women folk. Both male and female cook separately and eat separately. There is no feasting at the dormitory. The men folk would perform a ceremony known as Chong kapmei at the village gates. Chong kapmei means shooting at the effigy of man made of plaintain tree or other soft wood. The shooting of the effigy is a ceremony of omen taking and prophesy for the future. The young men throw a reed as spear to hit at the different parts of the effigy. For example, if the spear hits head of the effigy, the thrower will be successful in raids; if he hits of the effigy, it indicates successful hunting expedition; and he hits the belly of the effigy, it means a bountiful harvest.

There will be a hoi procession in which the whole men folk

shout ho ho in praise of Tingkao Ragwang. And in the village gate the elders will perform feats of Kabaomei (throwing challenge to the enemy) and Ritak ganmei (singing of war hymns). However no dancing and singing is performed. The youth of the village will perform competition in long jump and stone throwing. This will be followed by wrestling among the youths. The village Pei (council) will distribute Maru jou (wine of strength) to the gathering. The youths will produce new fire by friction of bamboo and wood (Mailapmei) and distribute to all the households. Every household will offer a sacrifice of fowl to Tingkao Ragwang. Rih Ngai purifies the village; segregation of men and women and separate cooking is the act of purification. It strengthens the mind, energy and devotion of the village to God.

Nanu Ngai

This festival is concerned with the community recognition of the children born in the previous year. It is a sort of the registration of these children in the house of the old women, Kengjapui Kaibang. Nanu Ngai literally means the festival of ear boring of the children born in the village. It is a three days festival. It is also a fertility festival for the birth of more children in the village. This covers the performance of the dances and songs, which are related with fertility. It is conducted by old men and old women. In the morning, the Najumgaimei rite is performed in the household where a child was born in the previous year. The Najumgaimei ceremony is performed in which an elder who has a living wife will act as a priest and offers one cock (Sangdai), hen (Sanglou), rice beer and ginger to Tingkao Ragwang for blessing to the child for longevity, success and a bright future. The priest performs Kasan Kanmei ritual and the ears of the children are bored in the house of Kengjapui. In the afternoon, they will perform a fertility dance known as Nanu Laam by the old women. It is of interest that a former British Political Agent in Manipur named William McCulloch records the

Nanu Ngai in his famous Account of the Valley of Munnipore and surrounding hill tribes (1859). He writes, "There is an annual village genna of three days in which the ears of the children born after the last festival of this nature are pierced". The last day of the festival is marked by a genna known as Nasang sanmei.

Lungnihai Rongmei of Thanagong village in Khoupum valley informs the author of the Nanu Ngai in the lower Rongmei area of Zeliangrong habitat. According to him, performance of this festival lasts for three days. This festival is celebrated in an elaborate way. The boys' dormitory (Khangchu) plays an important function in it. They would try to catch birds or fowls for the feeding (Nasam khang) of new born children in the families where the Nathanmei (celebration of new born child) occasion is celebrated. The dormitory would produce new fire by friction of wood and bamboo (Mairapmei) and distribute the same to the houses of families of new born children. The dormitory will present a basket of Chakhomjan (meat and eatables) to the houses of new born children where the Nathanmei ceremony is performed. Lungnihai explains the three days process of the Nanu festival prevalent in the villages of Khoupum valley.

Chakhomhamei: The first day is called Chakhomhamei in which the dormitory people present dry fish and meat to the families of the new born child (Nathankai). The family offers meal to the children of the village. They also offer a jar of rice beer and a bowl of chutney to the members of the dormitory. In the night, the boys of the dormitory sing song at the families of Nathankai praising the new born.

On the second day, in the morning the old women (Kengjapui) will fetch Nanudui (sacred water) and distribute to all the families of new born children. On that day, in the house of old women (Kengjapui Kaibang) will be performed the ceremony of ear piercing known as Jeisubon. The leaders of the dormitory will help the old women to pierce the ears of the children and decorate with earrings. They will pronounce, "From today, this child is member of my dormitory. No evil spirit will cast their evil eyes on you or touch you. Tingkao Ragwang will bless you".

In the families of new born child, the priest who has a living wife will perform the ceremony of Najumgaimei. This is also known as Nasan kanmei. The process is already described in the earlier section of this paragraph. The child will be bathed with Nanudui, the holy water of Nanu. After that every new born child will bring gifts to the house of old women (Kengjapui Kaibang). The gift item (Tamcha) consists of boiled roots, dry fish, dry meat, scented rice mixed with sesame, chicken meat and salt cakes. These items will be distributed to the elders and old women of the village. In the afternoon, there will be performance of dance and songs in the house of new born children. The family would offer rice beer and eatables to the boys and girls.

On the third day, the old women (Kengjapui) accompanied by old men will give blessings to the new born children. This is called Chathonmei. This will be followed by fertility songs and dances performed by old women and some children of the village.

Napkao Ngai

Nap kao literally means the calling of the paddy. It is a festival of worship of Tingkao Ragwang for successful cultivation and plentiful harvest. It is performed at the residence of Napmupou, the village functionary incharge of agricultural rites. A pig or a buffalo or even a mithun is sacrificed to Tingkao Ragwang. The liver of the animal sacrificed is cut into pieces and distribute to every household. The Napkao ceremony is performed in every household. Each family performs the ceremony by an offering of a fowl to Tingkao Ragwang for abundant harvest in the coming year. An important ritual is performed on this day which is called Napphun Keimei (seed sowing ceremony) in which a piece of land is excavated at the paddy field of the Napmupou and some paddy seeds are sowned therein. This ceremony is carried out by Napmupei, the wife of the Napmupou. The village elders will join the celebration by singing Laophunlu (seed sowing songs). After this festival the villagers are allowed to sow seeds at their respective paddy fields in jhum land.

Ginki Ngai (Entertainment of divine guests)

Ginki Ngai is a festival to mark the worship and entertainment of the goddess of paddy. The term Ginki means entertainment of the guest (in this context the guest is a divine goddess, therefore it is presume to be entertainmet of divine guest). This is a single day festival performed in the month of April or May in which women are to conduct the worship of the goddess of paddy known as Kangdailu. The myth connected with the worship of Kangdailu narrates that once Kangdailu appear in the form of an old woman, poor and unwanted, full of sores from head to toe. She went to every house of a village and requested for a night shelter. Nobody gave her shelter. Then she came to a house of two orphans. They told her that they had no extra room, food or cloth. They have nothing to offer as food. The old lady told the orphans that a grain of rice left over in their jar of grain might be cooked for her. The grain of rice multiplied and filled up the rice pot. The orphan boy got a crab out of her fishing basket and cooked the crab for the old woman. They found the cooking pot full with crabs. After eating, they went to sleep and they offer a bamboo mattress to sleep. That night, the old woman produced paddy grain for this poor family and she left. Later on it was found out that the old woman was no other thanthe goddess Kangdailu. The villagers requested her to come back but she refused. The villagers apologized to her for their misbehavior. Kangdailu asked them to perform the ceremony of entertaining the divine guest, Ginki. And later on the ceremony is performed every year. If ahe is worshipped, it is believed Kangdailu will bring rich harvest and prosperity. Thus Ginki has become a regular festival of the people.

Maleng (Gudui) Ngai

Maleng or Gudui Ngai is a popular festival of the Zeliangrong people performed after the completion of seed sowing in May or June. Maleng is a ritual performed in every household in which rice beer and ginger chutney are offered to Tingkao Ragwang, Supreme God and the goddess of paddy, Kangdailu. The performer of the ceremony is usually the head of the family or sometimes by village elder. The festival is also called Gudui as soup of ginger cooked with chicken curry is taken by the members of the family and distributed to the neighbours. Therefore these two rituals have been projected as representing a festival. The objective of the festival is to get a divine blessing for successful agricultural operation; a timely rainfall, successful growth of paddy plants, nourishing of the soil and prevention of insects and warding of pests and diseases. Maleng rite is followed by performance of Napkao (calling of paddy). In every household by the sacrifice of a cock it is believed that goddess Kangdailu is happy to see intestine of the cock being hung up at the door of the house and she blesses paddy to the family. The ginger soup mixed with chichen curry is served to every member of the family for health and longevity. In the afternoon there are entertainment programmes carried out by the boys and girls of the village. One is called Duidomphaimei, throwing of water in a plaintain leaf container and the other is Loijaimei (tug of war) between the boys and girls. The tug of war is believed to be a symbolic representation of contest between gods and goddesses for the possession of paddy. If the girls win, there will be plentiful harvest and if the boys win, there will be victory in the raids against the enemy. In the evening there will be singing of a song known as Katu which is an agricultural ritual song by marching across the village. On the next day, the village performed the Dikap Neih, abstaining from earth or muddy work. It is a sign that Zeliangrong people worship mother earth who is to be propitiated for hurting her and for fertility of the soil and prosperous harvest.

Tun Ngai (Festival of the rains)

Tun Ngai is the festival of rains during the rainy season, tun literally means rainy season. It is celebrated in the month of June-July. It lasts from 4 to 7 days. This festival has now fallen into bad days as the main purpose of the festival is to repair paths, ponds and clearing of jungles during the rainy season. This work is now being carried out by the government. Therefore importance of this festival has lost its relevance. Some villages still celebrate it for a single day. In Khoupum valley, this festival was once elaborately celebrated. The account given below by Lungnihai Rongmei is of historical value and social significance. This festival is also called Changkadaimei (repair of roads). However, the festival was performed in an institutionalized way through the boys' and girl's dormitory.

The first day of the Tun Ngai is marked by a ritual offering of holy wine to Tingkao Ragwang at the village gate where the youths start repairing the paths and culverts. The working team starts from the boys' dormitory by shouting the hohoing. The owner of the dormitory offers a jar of rice beer to the members of the dormitory. After the drinking of the rice beer, the youths of the dormitory sacrificed pig or cattle for feasting. The spleen of the pig was taken out for omen taking and the flesh of the pig are according to grade and status distributed to the elders and leaders of the dormitory. The chief priest and the highest age grade members of the village council known as Baanja were given the meat of the animals. The girls of the girls' dormitory led by their leaders came to the boys' dormitory and join in the cooking of the feast. The Khangbon group of the dormitory will prepare curry for the male members of the dormitory whereas elders incharge of girls will prepare curry for the girls. Then there will be a community feasting after hohoing shouts.

In the evening, the youths of the boys' dormitory will produce new fire and distribute the same to every household. And it will be followed by serving of wine to the elders. The boys and senior members of the boys' dormitory will bring gifts of eatables to the dormitory which will be inspected by the elders. Then the owner of the dormitory will present a jar of rice beer and a bowl of chutney which will be enjoyed by the members of the dormitory. There will be a choice of the best of the rice beer bamboo tumbler. And then the members of the girls' dormitory will present rice beer to the boys' dormitory. There will be song competition between the boys and girls at the girls' dormitory.

On the second day the boys and girls will perform Hangsenglaam (bamboo tube dance) at the house of the Gaanchang (Gaanchang kaibang). They will sing tun luh (rain songs), changchou luh (road making songs) in this dance.

On the third day, there will be feasting of the community at the dormitory where whatever is left is brought together and cooked. After feasting they will decide what to eat next year. It will be celebrated by shouting ho ho. The youths will go around the village singing Kairong lonluh (village guarding songs). Many obsevers including Dr. Robert Brown, a Political Agent of Manipur in the 19th century have referred to this festival. He said, "At a festival which occurs about July, they clear off jungle, the paths about their villages and leading to their fields – a most useful and necessary operation at that season of the year". Dr. Budha Kamei describes the Tun Ngai as "social service festival of the Zeliangrong community".

Ten Ngai (Bread Eating Festival)

It is a festival of entertainment among the youths of the village in which the girls collect rice for pounding flour to make bread and to make rice beer. It is an occasion in which the girls entertained the boys and other elders by offering them with rice bread. It is accompanied by a play known as Duidomngai in which water in the paintain leaf container is thrown among the boys and girls. It is also called Hoi Ngai because the whole people of the village participate in the shouting of Ho in praise of Tingkao Ragwang.

In the evening, after the rice bread being offered by the bread, there will be a song competition between boys and girls at the girls' dormitory. This Ten Ngai festival is purely a secular entertainment for young people.

Puakphat Ngai

It is a festival of agricultural recess. When the main cultivation of rice is over and early crops are ripened, the Puakphat Ngai is performed in the month of September. It is performed at the individual houses by offering a fowl to the Tingkao Ragwang by performing the paddy worshipping rite (Napkao Mei). In the past, there was community feasting in the dormitories. It is believed that whoever has not eaten fully in the feast of Puakphat will remain half starve during the coming months of the year. It is also performed by Liangmais and Zemes almost at the same time.

Dongjaomei

Dongjaomei literally means "seeing the granaries". It is a harvest festival, performed when the harvest is complete. The elders will visit every granary in the village and choose the two best granaries, full of paddy and vegetables. This is performed among the lower Rongmeis only and not a universal practice. The month of this festival is known as Dongjaobu, the month of seeing granary. In the former days of good harvest, Dongjaomei was a popular occasion. In Khoupum valley areas the elders of the Pei (village council) will choose the best two granaries after the harvest by shouting the Hoi and giving blessing to the owners. The villagers will sing a song known as Konsumei which is a song sung as a blessing. This month is also important as the performance of ceremonial sacrifices like Murengmei, Baalu and Matui is announced. Mostly during Dongjaomei, Murengmei ceremony is performed.

The agricultural ritual song known as the Lao hu kon will be sung. There, they will perform the Ri La Mei ceremony in which a pig will be sacrificed to God, the spleen will be examined as an omen indicator.

Chakak Ngai

It is a pre Gaan Ngai ritual festival performed for the preparation of the graves of the persons who died in the previous year. The hair of the children will be shaved off. There will be competition in stone throwing and long jump accompanied by the production of new fires and a Ho-Hoing procession in the village. On the last day, there will be performed the Ra Raimei (driving away of evil spirits and Shi Mun Tungmei) ceremony. Sacrifice of a dog, whose head with open jaw is put up at the village gate to bark away the evil spirits. Theis is similar with the Hekak Ngi of the Zeme. It sometimes continues for seven days, but is usually performed in a single day or is amalgamated with the Gaan Ngai festival (Gangmumei Kamei, p. 311).

Ritual ceremonies

Apart from the annual festivals described above, mention may be made of specific ritual ceremonies performed by the individual or dormitories which were once described by anthropologists as feast of merit. They are Taraang Kai, Baalu (Maku Baalu), Matui and Mureng ceremonies. Taraang Kai is the ritual construction of ornamented house dedicated to Tingkao Ragwang. Baalu sacrifices are ritual ceremonies dedicated to Tingkao Ragwang. Matui is also a religious ceremony performed by a dormitory to exhibit their achievements, wealth and solidarity, with thanks giving to the Supreme God. These ceremonies sustained the Zeliangrong culture, religion and way of life.

Zeliangrong dances

Talking about Zeliangrong festivals one naturally has to bring in the heritage of dances and music developed by Zeliangrong people. It is believed that their ancestors learned dancing and singing from the gods and creatures which attended the Jourumei of Amang (Jourube of Amangbow). Dances were performed and songs are sung under the supervision of a tortoise who was appointed Luhpou, song master. It is also mention that two men Gomtu and Gomning learnt dance from the Amang Jourumei ceremony. The myth of the origin of dance is narrated thus; all creatures are gathered at the ceremony of Amang. Each one of them performed a dance but one Longpu Gonpu was sleeping and he refused to wake up. A bull performed the dance first; a man performed beautiful dances, the tiger with his beautiful stripes of colour dance. A bear with his rough and hard hairs dance, so did the boar with his beautiful tusk. Yet Longpu Gonpu refused to wake up as he was aware of these dances. A cock putting on white cloth over his body and wings started dancing. Finally Longpu Gonpu said that he had not seen the dance of the cock and got up to see the dance. Though we do not have any authentic account of the dance it is known that dancing is a very old art form. Zeliangrong ancestors learnt dancing from gods, animals, birds and insects.

Forms of dances

The Zeliangrong dances have two main categories; (i) the ritual dances and (ii) the festival dances.

Ritual dances

Ritual dances are performed during the great ceremonies of Taraang, Baalu and Matui. The ritual dances include (a) Hoi laam, Male dance shouting ho ho as invocation to Tingkao Ragwang, (b)Joumon Kasukmei, Girls dance carrying wine bowls during Baalu sacrifice followed by group ritual dances, (c) Goipi Thenglam, dance of cutting the mithun head.

It may be mention that Hoi laam is an intricate dance form performed by the males both married and unmarried invoking God by shouting different refrains of Ho-hoing like Gan Hoi Laam, Kaiku Laam, Bangphen Laam and Ponsa Laam.

Joumon Kasukmei is a very important ritual dance form. It includes several dance forms, Jeisung Laam, Kaibon Sangmei, Kaibon Duimei, Banjai, Rih Lu, Muilu, and Khongphung.

The Festival dances

The festival dances are performed during the Gaan Ngai. They are of secular nature and in collectivity known as Chapa Laam which covers dances performed during special occasion. From the Chapa Laam dance masters have evolved several creative dance forms imitating the birds, animals and insects like Gaa Laam (Crab dance), Khoiguna Laam (Bee mating dance), Kit Laam (Cricket dance), Raengdai Laam (Hornbill dance), Guaichei Bang Laam (Bull horn dance), Apang Laam (Hoolok Gibbon dance) and Tareng Laam (Spinning dance).

Dance techniques

The Rongmei developed four dance techniques namely, Makhom Laam which originated from Marangjing (Makhom) village, Dinglian Laam, standing in rows, Phaicheng Laam, dance movement from left to right feet and Pheigoumei Laam, waving dance cloths by standing.

Musical instruments and dance costumes

The musical instruments of the festivals including Gaan Ngai festival include the following.

i. Horns of mithun, cattle and buffalo
ii. Drum, cymbal
iii. Harps known as Raa
iv. Gong (Semmu)

Male costumes

a. Folded Mareipan: From shoulder to the knees
b. Langsem: decorated breast band
c. Songnai: A red colour kilt from waist to the knee
d. Renglan: A long coloured kilt from waist to knee
e. Pheilak and Senlam: Waist belts
f. Pheidom and Phaikam: Calf covers

Male ornaments

a. Jeisu: Earring made of the feathers of Jeisu bird
b. Banpomta: Armlet made of elephant tusk
c. Gang Kam: Necklace made of conch shell
d. Nathang: An armlet made of copper

Female costumes and ornaments

a. Pikhim and sanadong: head dress
b. Beithing Lem: Earring decoration
c. Tadantu: Cornelian beads
d. Tadu: Brass armlets
e. Nathang: Brass bracelets
f. Langhu Pheisoi: Female sarong
g. Phang Phei: Black cloth covering the upper part of the body
h. Phailaak: Waist band

Dancers of Hangrum, Assam

Dancers of Peren, Nagaland

Dancers of Imphal, Manipur

Dancers of Gaan Ngai, Manipur

Zeme dancer of Manipur

Rih Laam: A Youth in the costume of War Dance

Elders at Ngai Kai (Festival House) at Chingmeirong, Manipur

Drummers of Intuma (Nagaland) (Reproduced from Milada Ganguly, 1984)

5
Gaan Ngai, A Winter Festival

The Gaan Ngai is the greatest festival of the Zeliangrong people. This is called Hega Ngi among the Zeme speakers, Chaga Ngi or Chaga Gadi among the Liangmai speakers and Gaan Ngai proper among the Rongmei speakers. Gaan Ngai literally means the festival of winter season (Gaan or Ganh means winter or dry season and Ngai means festival). Many scholars belonging to the Zeliangrong community have profusely written on the Gaan Ngai festival. The Gaan Ngai Celebration Committee, Manipur in 2003 published a book entitled, Gaan-Ngai: A festival of Zeliangrong people. A section of this book is a collection of articles on Gaan Ngai festival written by six scholars namely, Gangmumei Kamei, Lanbilung Gonmei, Late Lanlimei Kamson, Meiphunlung Thaimei, Makulim Remei and K.C. Kabui (Lanbipu). This is a well written comprehensive account of the festival. In 2004, Prof. Gangmumei Kamei in his "A History of the Zeliangrong Nagas: From Makhel to Rani Gaidinliu" deals among other things, the festivals of the Zeliangrong Nagas including Gaan Ngai, Chaga Ngi and Hega Ngi. The comparative study of these festivals clearly proves the commonality and same origin of these festivals. The Zeliangrong Heraka association, North East India based at Haflong published a very useful treatise entitled, "Zeliangrong Customary Laws" in 2009. This work gives an account of the Zeliangrong Heraka festivals as practiced among the Zeme and Liangmai speakers who followed the faith. This work gives a comprehensive description of the Hega Ngi festival. The man behind this important publication is Pautanzan Newme, the General Secretary of the Zeliangrong Heraka Association of North East India. Another work named, "Heraka: The primordial religion and its revitalization movement" (2011) deals with the festivals performed by the Heraka followers including the Hega Ngi. It deals with the songs and dances and several ceremonies followed by them. The two publications gave a comprehensive account of the Hega Ngi festival. Though the Liangmai speakers have claimed to have given up the Chaga Ngi festival, some of their scholars continue to write on the Chaga Ngi festival. Mention may be made of a paper written by Kaikhamang Daimei, a former Director of Tribal research Institute, Manipur on Chagah festival and its significance. He describes the Chaga festival as the most celebrated festival of the Liangmais. Achenbou Nuimai, General Secretary of Liangmai Aruang Dimapur writes on Chaga Gadi festival and its significance in Nagalnad Post, Dimapur dated 30th October 2010 on the occasion of Chaga Gadi festival. He describes Chaga Gadi festival is one of the most celebrated festivals of the Zeliangrongs, Liangmai in particular. Tunchapbo S.P. wrote on Chaga Gadi on the same day. In another publication on 1st November 2011, Tunchapbo S.P. wrote a sensible paper entitled, "Post modern understanding of Chaga Gadi for social transformation".

In 2010, Chaoba Kamson wrote "The Philosphy of Gaan Ngai" in English and some chapters were written in Rongmei. This book gives the genesis of Gaan Ngai festival, its meaning and the different stages of the festival and the purpose of the festival. This has increased our knowledge of the Gaan Ngai as explained by the author. Another publication was brought out in 2012 by the State Level Gaan Ngai Celebration Committee, Manipur. Two papers were published in this book entitled, "Gaan-Ngai: Festivity among the Zeliangrong of North East India". The first article is entitled, Ritual festival of Zeliangrong written by Dr. Budha Kamei, a research scholar and the second article is entitled, Chakaan Gaan Ngai: The living religious and cultural festival was written by Chaoba Kamson. These two papers are highly documented and their accounts are very authentic. Dr. Budha Kamei tries to give a comprehensive account of the Zeliangrong festival whom he called Ngi to describe the festivals of the three sections of the Zeliangrong community. Chaoba gives the ritualistic aspects of the Gaan Ngai festival.

These publications have greatly increased our knowledge of the festival of Gaan Ngai, Hega Ngi and Chaga Ngi. The following account is presented separately on each one of the festivals.

Hega Ngi

Hega Ngi is a Zeme festival equivalent to the Gaan Ngai. Now with the growth of Heraka cult it is regarded as the main festival of the Zeliangrong Heraka cult. It is performed on the 13th day of lunar month of Pousa in December – January. Now the date of the festival is on this same day when Gaan Ngai is also performed. In 2012, the year of my research the Hega Ngi was performed on 7th January 2012 when the Gaan Ngai was also performed in Manipur, Assam and Nagaland.

Ursula Graham Bower, a British freelance anthropologist who engaged herself in anthropological study of the Zemes during the World War II describes Hega Ngi as a Zeme New Year Feast. She gives an interesting account of Hega Ngi. She writes, "H(e)gangi began a few days later. This great feast marks the turn of the year. It opens with the parting of the dead from the living; with its main day, Hgangi itself, the old year closes and the new begins; during its course, huge, stylized wooden effigies–are set up at the gates to the village, and ceremonially speared by the men and the boys – a relic of human sacrifies; and the various religious ceremonies, omen takings and holidays run on for a full fortnight" (Bower, Naga Path, 1950, London, p. 99)

The Hega Ngi festival is divided into three parts. The first part is known as Kachimangi in which five days are devoted to the observation of religious rituals for those who died in the previous year. Tingkupeu, the priest worshipped the Tingwang with fowls and other items like ginger. Offerings are made on the graves of the dead. The priest distributes grains to all households. The second part is called Hekak Ngi, parting ceremony of the dead from the village. The villagers are engaged during Hekak Ngi in the making of the graves, stone pulling ceremony if any, erection of wooden poles and raising of stone slabs over the graves. After the Hekak Ngi is over, the village priest and elders perform a ritual to drive away the evil spirits from the village. This is the third part of the festival and is called Heragnabe.

Heraka Hega Ngi

In modern times, with the reforms of the Heraka cult, the Hega Ngi is performed according to their guidelines. Zeliangrong Customary Laws (2009) says, "Out of the five major festivals, Hega' ngi festival is the biggest festival of Zeliangrong people. It is observed in the month of Ndui or Kere keu (December or January). Hega' ngi literally means Hega (Boon or good luck) and it is also called the year ending festival. It is believed that those people whosoever get chance to observe Hega' ngi festival is considered to be the luckiest person, who could succeed in all his/her cultivating works of the year by the blesings of the Almighty Tingwang (Supreme God). As such, the first day of the festival is observed as the

Tingwang Mpua peibe mai (offering day of newly cultivated crops to Almighty Tingwang)... (In Lodiram viallge the author found the observance of the first day by feasting in the individual houses in the evening. It was also found that the Government of Assam had declared the first day of Hega Ngi as a general holiday in the Dima Hasao district. Functions were organized in which invitees from other communities are welcomed and entertained in the feast and followed by dance and songs).

"The second day is observed as 'Ngidi mai' (the main festival day). It is the day of the sports such as, long jump, shot put, wrestling etc. all the aged men and young men with full traditional attires march in procession doing 'Rehoi' (shouting). It starts from the lower side of the village and march to the upper side and then from upper to lower side of the village. People lastly stop 'Rehoi' at the HEZUADEKUNG (jumping ground of the village). There they start longjump and then do shot put. After completion of sports, all spectators enjoy the festival feast in groups. (The winners in the longjump and shot put competition will be given blessings by the elders and the winner will in turn present gifts of cloths particularlt kilt to the elders which is now substituted by money)

"On the third day of the festival it is observed as 'the Puapatmai' (day of merry making, eating and drinking festival feast). This day is also observed by villagers marching village procession with full customary dresses as usual and to proceed towards the maximum harvest owner's house in the village (Nteutuaki) and then to 'Nteu-nraikak ki' (the host house for consecrating service on a particular selected boy of the village by the priest).

"As per Zeliangrong customary laws, following works should be done completely before the observation of Hega' ngi festival:

1. Parting ceremonial service to the souls of the dead from the village.
2. Making of the graves of the dead (if any)
3. Erection of memorial stone or installation of wooden pole as a mark of more cultivation of crops from amongst the villagers

Hega' Ngi Ritual

1. Hoisting of flag at Kelumki early in the morning (at sun rise)
2. Collection of Tingwangmpua at Kelumki (offering of newly cultivated crops to Almighty Tingwang)
3. The priest performs worship upon the offering of Tingwangmpua by the villagers
4. Entering into the Kelumki singing the devotional song either by 'Tingkao Ragwang or Duisuna'
5. Individual prayers at the alter
6. Singing a prayer song of 'I lukeni gai maite'
7. The remaining programme is followed up as usual like that of the Full Moon day.

Hega Ngi festival has been now simplified by the religious authorities of the Heraka Association.

Chaga Ngi (Chaga Gadi)

Chaga Ngi is the earliest form of post harvest festival performed by the Zeliangrong people when they were living in Makuilongdi. Despite the migration of Zeme speakers and Rongmei speakers from Makuilongdi and establishment of their separate settlements where they performed their Hega Ngi or Gaan Ngai, the original settlers continued to perform Chaga Ngi. Chaga means festival and Chaga Ngi is the most celebrated festival of the Liangmai speakers of

Zeliangrong community. Several Rongmei speaking villages in the Trans Barak basin perform Chaga Ngi. Recently, the Liangmais start calling the Chaga Ngi as Chaga Gadi. An interesting write up on Chaga Ngi is published by a scholar named, Tunchapbo S.P. His article is reproduced in the form of paraphrasing.

Chaga Ngi (or Chaga Gadi) is the biggest festival of the Liangmai community. It comes annually in the month of October. This month is called Chaga hiu, the month of Chaga. It is a festival of war and merry making. It is also a festival of purification, sanctification and rededication. Nowadays, this festival is celebrated every year on 30th October which is celebrated to express a cultural showcase marked by grand feast and dances. In the past as a preparation for the Chaga festival people go hunting, fishing and trapping of birds in search of delicious food stuffs. During the festival there was a practice that married men and women were to drink and eat from banana leaves while the unmarried men and women were to eat and drink from bamboo cups and plates.

Both men and women have to use separate hearth in making food inorder to purify themselves. It was a taboo to have relation between male and female during the festival. During the Chaga Ngi men will not sleep with their wives. They are to maintain discipline by not touching anything of woman. It is believed that if the men folk failed to maintain discipline, bad luck follows them in the war. So men folk are to discipline themselves and not to defile themselves by impurity. In order to make themselves aloof from women, men would spend their time at the male dormitory (Khangchiuki). There was a strong prohibition for the boys to visit the girls. Same restriction was imposed on the girls who are to spend in their dormitory (Luchiuki). They enjoyed best foods and drinks during the Chaga festival.

The festival lasts for five days. According to Tungchapbo, the following daily activities of the festival are followed. He writes,

"Day one: It begins with 'Chamimalapbo' (making fire) which is also called 'day of welcome'. On this day, they had to start their hearth with fresh firewood for cooking. On this very night they are to eat their choicest food to see their eyes bulging in the morning. As they finish drinking and eating they gather up in their Khangchiuki with the elders to crack jokes and sing songs. On this day the children also gather their own chaga rooster competing in sizes and strength.

Day two: Next day is the day of 'Npengkiapbo' (shooting of human effigy), early in the morning the selfless boys (chaliumabomai) voluntarily go to the jungle to cut the tree for Npeng (effigy). Npeng is cut by those whose parents are still alive and those who live a pure and holy life. They are to go for cutting only after being blessed by their parents. Npeng has to made in resemblance to human being. Chicken feathers are placed on the head of Npeng and also eye, nose, mouth, ear, neck, heart and chest has to be marked with a black colour. After everything is done, Npeng is tied on the top of the pole or post.

Keeping themselves pure and holy and with a loud ho-hoing proclaiming their forefather's name, Npeng is shot with an arrow. Certain features are made on the spot where they could hit : if it happens to hit on the head – the enemy die of head pain; if on the neck – the one who shoot s will have plenty of rice; if on the heart – the enemy will die with much trouble; if on the right chest – the enemy will die in war; and if on the left chest – the on ewho shoots will win many girls. If anyone can't hit Npeng then the Tingkupao (priest) will take the Npeng stick (arrow) by hand and put it in the feet of Npeng as a sign of surrender. Those whose relatives died in the previous year are not to shhot Npeng. After shooting of

Npeng, every boy goes back to their Khangchiu...ho-hoing. Everyone eats delicious foods and drinks abundantly. Eating and drinking was followed by dancing.

Day three: The following day was the day of gadi which was also called (sharing of meals, food and drinks) where everyone is expected to come with their best attire for the mega feast.

Day four: This day was called 'Chaga pabo'. On this day all the left over food and drinks are distributed to the elderly people. The festival is so fascinating that young boys and girls are reluctant to end up the festival.

At the end of the festival, they washed their hands and mouth. They sing songs and make merry. All go around the village and back to their own respective houses. By then boys can go the girls and the married men and women are no more restricted to be with each other.

Day five: This day is particularly for lderly people who continued to drink and eat the left over food and drinks which is called Zauba (eating left over)...Till zauba is finished up it is a taboo to do any domestic work" (Tunchapbo S.P., Chaga Gadi, Nagaland post, 30th October, 2010).

As noted earlier the Chaga Ngi festival has been secularized by the Christian Liangmais. However those who follow the indigenous religion observed the festival. A Liangmai writer and scholar, Tasile N. Zeliang explains that Chaga Ngi is still observed by the Zeliang of Nagaland. Deralung Nren of Jalukie who originally came from Boupungwa, Peren district confirms that Chaga is observed by them. During the Chaga festival, there were procession of the youths across the village shouting ho-ho. It is followed by a sporting competition in long jump, stone throwing and wrestling. It is reported that in their villages on the fifth day the boys are free to go out for hunting, fishing etc. On the sixth day there is a genna. The villagers get together in their traditional attires and no one goes out of the village.

So the Chaga Ngi or Chaga Gadi is observed by the Christian Liangmais in a secular form while among the followers of indigenous religion, the traditional festival is followed with great devotion. The Christian scholars are in favour of observing the Chaga Gadi adopting the social and moral values but excluding the ritualistic aspect. Tunchapbo argues that Chaga Ngi means sharing. One outstanding feature of the traditional culture of the Liangmai is found in the principle of sharing one's resources generously with others whatever one has. Sharing is a Liangmai cultural values...If we reflect this sharing, it is equivalent to love in action which is against selfishness, exploitation, corruption and misappropriation...Chaga Ngi teaches us 'sharing'. He concludes "Today to construct relevance of Chaga Ngi we must critically analyze the past religio-culture and tradition with the purpose of rediscovering and discerning its message...This led the present generation greatly influenced by outside culture that today majority of our people do not know the importance of one's culture...He pleads that 'the present Liangmais can continue to celebrate Chaga Ngi with new perspectives by honouring God in their respective places crossing denominational and religious barriers giving corporate new identity as a Liangmai and as a Christian" (Tunchapbo S.P., Post modern understanding of Chaga Gadi fro social transformation, Nagaland Post, 1st November, 2011). Perhaps what he says is an appeal to all the Zeliangrong people who have left their religion and culture.

Gaan Ngai

The Gaan Ngai festival is being presented in this chapter on different aspects presented as follows.

The Genesis

According to a Zeliangrong myth as reproduced by Chaoba Kamson in his Philosophy of Gaan Ngai, Tingkao Ragwang the Supreme God created a god named Tingpurengsonang. He was made a patriarch of common dormitory of gods, men, animals and all creatures. They spoke a common language. The duty of Tingpurengsonang was to teach men to speak, sing and way of life. They celebrated a festival at that time. There was a conflict and tension between men and gods. At that time if men attended first at male dormitory, men controlled over gods and if gods attended the dormitory first, they controlled men. As men's intellect increased day by day, gods became jealous of the rise of men and started killing them. Men complained to Tingpurengsonang that they could not live with the gods as they (gods) killed men. The patriarch of the dormitory pacified men stating that men did not yet learn the language, songs, mode of worship etc. so they should continue to live together. Men obeyed the patriarch and continued to live in common dormitory. He taught men the divine tactics to kill gods by cutting the main ceremonial post of dormitory with a sword. Gods also complained to the patriarch that they wanted to live separately from men. Tingpurengsonang consoled the gods but they rejected his plea. Finally the patriarch made his judgement that men and gods will live separately and speak different language, eat different foods, drink, way of life etc.

The patriarch of the male dormitory taught men the knowledge of cultivation, culture, mode of worship etc. In course of time, men started cultivation and harvest bountiful crops. Then men began to celebrate Gaan Ngai festival as a thanks giving to Tingkao Ragwang for the good harvest with the oblation of holy wine to Him, performance of religious, cultural and customary activities thus bringing peace and unity among men. With the direction of the patriarch, men offered foods and drinks to Tingkao Ragwang invoking Him for longevity of life and prosperity for the coming year. They also offered food and drinks on the graves for the departed souls.

Seeing the observance of Gaan Ngai festival with pomp and gaiety, gods approached the patriarch to allow them to participate in the festival. At first instance He rejected their request. After pleading again and again He accepted their request. The patriarch called the men and told them to blow the horn of mithun or cattle either at male dormitory or jumping ground. This was an invitation to all kind of gods to participate in the Gaan Ngai festival. He also advised gods to give blessings to mankind in return. Further He ordered men to perform a ritual called Ralen Loumei (worship of all gods of Zeliangrong pantheon) on the last day of the festival at the northern gate of the village by a priest. Accordingly men performed worship of seven brothers of gods of worldly Ragwang, surrounding gods, presiding deities and propitiate evil spirits to distance from mankind. It is believed that gods are escorted up to the norther gate of the village on the last day of the festival. Since then Zeliangrong people have been performing the Ralen Loumei ceremony on the last day of the festival. Thus it is believed that Gaan Ngai festival had evolved from the house of Tingpurengsonang. This is a mythical expalination of the origin of Gaan Ngai therefore it may or may not be authentic. However the evolution of Gaan Ngai from the Zeliangrong settlement at Makuilongdi and migration to three directions where they evolve Gaan Ngai in varying ways was a historical development.

Celebrating the Gaan Ngai

Gaan Ngai is a post-harvest festival. Therefore in the past it was observed in the month of October. However in 1947 the Zeliangrong community leaders decided that it be held on the 13th day of the Meitei month of Wakching which tallies with Pousa month of Sakabda of the Indian era. After long persuasion, the Zeliangrong people now perform Gaan Ngai on the same day in the states of Manipur, Nagaland and Assam. The Government of Manipur declared Gaan Ngai as a general holiday since 1998 while the Government of Assam declared it as a restricted holiday in the district of Cachar (in the district of Dima Hasao of Assam, Hega Ngi is a general holiday on this day while Chaga Ngi or Chaga Gadi is a holiday on 31st October in Nagaland). The coming of the Gaan Ngai is announced on the first day of the month of Wakching/Pousa by blowing the horn of mithun or cattle. This is called Gaan Shanmei. The Gaan Ngai is also celebrated as worship of God for giving to men good harvest and expression of thanks giving of man to God.

A writer gives a beautiful environment of the approach of Gaan Ngai festival. He writes, "When the chilly breezes sweep through the bare bark of the winter trees and sky turns bluer and higher... when the barns are full and pumpkins and yam plumped, while the dead of the year has not left for the land of the dead, when he still sleeps in the grave dark, the 'Gaan Ngai' days arrive thrilling the hearts of the living of the coming celebration – hastening the weavers to finish their new shawls, youths practicing dance steps to the beats of the drums as every step anticipates the festival of the living and the dead" (Meiphunlung Thaimei, Gaan Ngai, 2003, Imphal).

In several villages instead of blowing of the horn, an elder goes around the whole length and breadth of the village and shouts out the message of the coming of the Gaan Ngai. However there are variations from village to village. Kathuna Daimei of Chingmeirong Rongmei village informed the author that the announcement of Gaan Ngai was done four days before the main day of the festival. It is called Ngai Nit kaopatmei (announcement of the festival day).

With the announcement of the Gaan Ngai day, youths of the dormitory prepare the jumping ground where will be held the competition of long jump and stone throwing. The owners of the dormitories particularly wife of the owner prepare rice beer for the coming festival. The members of the dormitory divided into several age grades, Khangbon, Gaanpi, and Shingkhangloi gather fire wood for the dormitory.

The eve of Gaan Ngai festival

On the eve of the festival, the village elder informs the villagers to prepare vegetables for feasting on the festival day. The women folk (Mathenmei) of the village will organiz a feast for themselves on this day. This feast is called Mathenmei Jeitumei. The youths of the village will bring the firewood to their respective dormitories (this is called Thingtinmei, coming with the firewood). The leaders of the dormitory will inspect the preparation made for the performance of the festival next day particularly, materials for the production of new fire, the drums, the stone or iron shot puts and bamboo (Goo) for making of the head dress of the elders. The leaders of the dormitory will enforce discipline and order in the functioning of the dormitory by giving instructions to the members. The Gaan Ngai is regarded as a festival marking the end of the year; therefore it has been popularly presumed to be a New Year festival. Gaan Ngai means festival of winter season; and so it is performed in this season meaning that it is a festival of dry or winter season. This festival also marks the parting of the dead from the living. Ceremonies are performed to give farewell to the dead souls. It is believed that before the performance of the Gaan Ngai festival, the spirits of the dead who died in the previous year are still hovering in the houses of their parents or relatives. It is believed that Gaan Ngai separates the living from the dead and this is a festival of the living.

Ngai Gangmei (Opening day of the festival)

Gaan Ngai festival is based on the worship of the Supreme God, Tingkao Ragwang by the Zeliangrong people. The whole culture, religion and social life are interwoven in the performance of the Gaan Ngai which sustains the life style of the Zeliangrong people.

The opening day of the festival is called Ngai Gangmei (coming of the festival). A series of ceremonies are performed on the opening day. It starts with the omen taking ceremony (Daan jaomei) as the day breaks, being performed at the abode of the village deity (Bambu) in the northern gate of the village, and performed by the village priest by the offering of egg and ginger. The priest will perform divination by ginger to know the future.

It is followed by a Sacrifice offered to Tingkao Ragwang at the boys' dormitory. The whole village elders and all the members of the dormitory will gather at their dormitory known as Khangchu. The girls will also gather at their dormitory known as Luchu. The whole village community will sacrifice an animal to the Supreme God, Tingkao Ragwang. The animal may be a mithun or a boar. A healthy youth will be entrusted to kill the boar by hitting of the animal by a wooden mortar or spearing the mithun which is bound into a wooden post. After the sacrifice of the boar, village elders who are experts in the examination of the spleen will inspect it for the omen of the year. The flesh of the boar will be ceremonially distributed to the various functionaries of the male dormitory and other elders of various grades. The male dormitory will give a portion of the meat to the girls' dormitory. In the dormitory the elders and members will partake a curry cooked with the insides of the boar and its blood. This is known as Jeitumei, the feast of insides of the animal cooked with its blood. Nowadays the feast entertains all the village folk with the meat and the rice presented by the dormitory. The feasting would be preceded by invocation to God known as Hoi kaomei (ho-hoing). There are different styles of Hoi kaomei namely, Rihai hoi, Hoitan hoi, etc. Naplao Hoi is performed before every community meal at the dormitory.

Gaan Ngai is also a festival in which the physical might of the youth of the village is demonstrated. The youths will prepare for the competition of long jump and stone throwing at the village jumping ground, Daanshaanpung. In the afternoon the whole menfolk go out into a procession ho-hoing, known as Hoi gammei procession. Every male, the elders, married males, unmarried male even children putting on best ceremonial attires, holding spears participate in the Hoi gammei procession. It starts from the boys' dormitory, proceed to the village gates shouting ho-ho, then to the village jumping ground. The youth participates in the competition in stone throwing, long jump and wrestling which are carried out in presence of the whole community. Stone throwing and long jump will be inaugurated by an elder. Those youth who win in the competition will be blessed by the elders and they in turn will give gifts to the elders by presentation of their clothes. In modern times it has been substituted by money payment. It is a very beautiful philosophy of the Zeliangrong people, the winner, the victorious and the successful will entertain the community for the blessing on them for future success.

The procession proceeds to the boys' dormitory and the selected youths will produce new and sacred fire by the method of wood and bamboo friction. Then the fire will be distributed to every household with which the women folk will start the fire in their hearths. The production of fire is called Mailapmei. Because of this production of new fire, some ignorant persons described the Gaan Ngai festival as the festival of light. There is no lighting in the village on the opening day of the festival.

Every household will perform a sacrifice by an offer of a fowl to Tingkao Ragwang as a thanks giving for good harvest. They perform the worship as Nap Kaomei (calling of paddy). The hosewives will offer ginger, rice beer, cooked rice and liver of the fowl at the hearth. This is called Nap Chanmei to the deities presiding over the hearth.

The village elders will go around the village and give warning to every household to enjoy the Gaan Ngai and not to indulge in quarrels among the family members failing which will be punished by the village council. The youth of the dormitories would come together in a common place for sharing of the food brought from their respective houses. After the meal, the youths would go out in groups singing village guarding song (Kairong lonlu) throughout the night. Thus ends the first day of Gaan Ngai festival.

Ngai Dai (The main festival)

Ngai Dai meaning the great festival is performed on the second day of Gaan Ngai. This day is also known as Tamchan Ngai as the members of the dormitory will present gift of eatables to their respective dormitories for their respective feastings. Sometimes the members of the boys' dormitory and the families of those unfortunate youth who passed away the previous year will present the Tamcha (gift in the form of food, eatables, drinks, meat and rice) to their respective dormitory for partaking by the members. The parents of the dead members give the Tamcha in remembrance of their deceased near and dear ones.

In the evening, the girls will perform the Tamchan dance in the offices of the various institutions namely, Pei (village council), Kengjapui Kaibang (office of old women), Gaanchang kaibang (office of elders) and Napmu Kaibang (the house of the functionary of agricultural rites). This dance is known as Tamchan laam (Tam means chutney of vegetables, Chan means request and Laam means dance). The purpose of the Tamchanmei is to go around and offer worship in the four institutional offices not to cause any illness or disease to the youths. If there is no dance on this occasion there is usually a singing competition between the boys' and girls' dormitories.

Tuna Gaan Ngai

Tuna Gaan ngai literally means the festival of the youth. This day is important for the dead and living and for the strength and prosperity of the village.

i. The dormitories will perform Thei-Kadi Laam (Dance in honour of the dead) at the selected families in which death occurs in the previous year. The family will prepare the graves of the dead to whom offering in form of food and drink will be made. The dead will be given a ritual farewell in the form of dance.

ii. The dormitories perform Khangbo Kadi Laam, a dance in honour of Khangbon, the heads of the dormitory who are being promoted to a higher post of Gaanchang.

iii. The dormitories will perform a farewell dance in honour of girls who are going to be married in the coming season.

There are two individual rituals to be performed by the heads of the founder clans of the village. This ritual is abandoned because of the conversion of the heads of the villages into Christianity. This is also not held in Manipur valley where villages are built up by purchase of lands from the Meitei owners. There was no necessity of creating a new village in a barren mountain. The two rites performed on this day are:

Rangteng pammei (ritual of reaffirmation)

Rangteng pammei literally means embracing the village gate. On this day or on the eve of Long ruimei (hill trekking) when there is no dancing, a ceremony known as the Rangteng pammei is performed by the heads of the founder clans of the village. This is a ceremony to strengthen and confirm the village gates, an act of reaffirmation of the strength and unity of the village against the elements and forces inimical to the village.

At night, when there is complete silence in the village, the Rangteng pammei ceremony will be performed. During the day time, a wooden pole will be prepared, the gaa creepers and canes will be collected by the youth and kept in the village gates. In the night, the wooden pole of the village gate is raised by the head or an elder of the settler's clan which is the family of the Rangteng pammei at the right side of the village ans with appropriate hymns chanted. (It is not to ne audible to the gathering).

Two youths dressed in ceremonial warrior dress, holding dao and spear cut the village gate pole (Rangteng Khumei). It is followed by the Ho-Hoing of the gathering to scare away the wild beasts and evil elements followed by a complete silence. The two youths report to the elder, "Our village is protected and safe, it will be prosperous". The gathering at the village gate will respond by shouting "gaiye, gaiye, gaiye, gaiye (meaning good four times). Then the Ho-Hoing and again the response of "gaiye" four times. From the village gate, the gathering proceeds shouting Hoi to the village jumping ground. Then the refrain of "gaiye, gaiye, gaiye, gaiye" will be repeated and it is over. They return to the dormitories in a Hoi procession.

Khunnummei (offering at the hole of the village gate)

In the afternoon of the day, the head of the settlers' clan of the village known as Nampou (owner of the village), the chief functionary will go to the village gates and dig holes in which he offers an egg and iron pieces with the chanting of hymns. It is an affirmation that he is the descendent of the founder of the village and prays for the affirmation of his position and strength of the village. This has social and administrative significance. It is the reassertion of the chiefship of the head of the settler's clan which should be accepted by everybody in the village.

On this day of the festivals, the traditional dances of different pattern will be performed by the youth (boys and girls). On this day, the dance, merry making, songs of the Zeliangrong are performed. The essence of the aesthetic sense of the Zeliangrong people and their culture are found expression in a grand form (Gangmumei Kamei, Gaan Ngai, 2003, pp. 5-6; See also Dr. Budha Kamei, Ritual Festivals of Zeliangrong, 2012, pp 13-14).

Longkumei (Hill trekking)

The fourth day, Dr. Budha Kamei writes, "This day is called Longruimei (Longkumei) meaning hill trekking; (Long means hill, Ruimei means trekking). On this day, the boys and girls under the auspices of village elders perform Longruimei in a nearby mountain range. On the top of the hill, they will show their talents and capabilities of the lifetime achievements. Khong Baimei, drum beating is carried out by those who are expert in the art. Those who were the killers of enemy, tiger, bear, python, wild pig etc. show Kabaomei (warrior talks). The boys offer girls, sing traditional songs called Luchenlu (lamenting song) and eat the Gaktingtam (boiled pork pounded with salt, ginger, chillies and made into balls) with drink. Among them, two boys and girls are chosen to be kings and queens and each of them wears a crown made of Fak, a kind of grass. The boys and girls are known as Fakgwangs and at the end shouting Hoi is performed. In the evening they return to the village and perform Phakgwang

Lam, dance in front of the houses of the Phakgwangs. The participants are entertained with eatables and drink".

Longkumei is a very beautiful aspect of Gaan Ngai festival. In some villages it is very elaborately organized. In the village of Chingmeirong, Kathuna Daimei and Makulim Remei state that "On this occasion, the village youth under the care of elders go out for an outing (Ram phaangmei) to neighbouring hill or hillocks. They carry with them the choicest foods and drinks. They sing songs and collect Pongring, a plant with luscious green leaves and bearing berry like red fruit (Ilex sp.). The fruits are used especially for Daan Sanmei (omen taking) to know their fortune. They make wreaths with the leaves and present it to the elders. Pongring actually is one ingredient of the seven medicinal plants which when combined make a very powerful medicine. This combination is often called the Elixir of Life. This is used by the Muhs (priests) of the Zeliangrong community. In the evening they beautify themselves (youths) with the leaves and fruits of Pongring and dance admist much rejoicing" (Makulim Remei, Gaan Ngai: A multi-faceted festival, 2003, pp. 45-46)

Napchanmei (worship of goddess of wealth)

Napchanmei is the closing day of the Gaan Ngai festival. This day is meant for the worship of Kangdailu, the goddess of foodgrain. It is also regarded as a day of prayer to goddess of wealth Kambuipui. During the past four days of the festival, there has been wastage due to lavish use of eatables. To call back the wealth wasted, the goddess who lived in the form of the hearth stones in the house is worshipped. On this day, a ceremony known as Napkao (calling of the paddy) is performed at the dormitories of the boys and girls, Khangchu and Luchu to restore the consumed and wasted rice during the festival invoking Tingkao Ragwang and Kangdailu.

The priest of the village performs the Napkaomei ritual at the boys' dormitory with the offering of a boar and a fowl. On this day, the youth of the boys' dormitory distribute a bamboo tube of wine to every household and the bamboo tube is hung in the front wall of the house. The purpose of hanging of the bamboo is to "store" the epidemic diseases inside the bamboo tube. It will be thrown away outside the western gate of the village. It is believed that such a practise of warding of the diseases shows that east will bring life and west will bring death. This practice appears to be a superimposed one.

In every household there will be worship of goddesses of food grain and wealth. The housewives will offer a liver, cooked rice and rice beer to the goddesses namely Kambuipui, Charaipui and Kairao. At the dormitory there will be feasting of the elders and members of the institution. After the feast is over, there will be assembly of singing together- moking, joking and praising. They visit the girls' dormitory and join a singing competition with the girls. It lasts throughout the night.

Raangpatmei (worship of all deities of the pantheon)

After the Gaan Ngai festival is over, the village community performs the worship of all the gods of Zeliangrong pantheon on the day of Raangpatmei which literally means going beyond the village gate. On this day the ritual of Raren loumei, performance of the sacrifices to seven brother gods and other deities worshipped in a particular village is observed at the abode of the presiding deity in the northern gate (Kaipi Bambu). When Raren loumei is performed, the village observed a Neihmei, the village gates are closed and nobody's allowed to enter the village. Since all the deities are worshipped in this ritual, every household will contribute a fowl, ginger, chilies, turmeric, salt and plaintain leaves to the village council. The priest or Taku of the village will perform the sacrifices by chanting appropriate hymns. The deities worshipped in the Raren loumei are divided into two; the seven brother gods and an unhatch deity named Dimei, and the other groups of deities which represent nature and deities around the village. The brother gods of Zeliangrong pantheon are given in the following:

1. Ragwang: The king of the gods of the earth (Lower Realm) also known as Na-Ragwang.
2. Bisnu (Manchanu/ Buisnu/ Bonchanu): The most powerful god on earth who looks after the affairs of men, nature and animals and communicates with men through the medium of priest.
3. Napsinmei (Laorang): The god of paddy
4. Chonchai: Adverse to wine, he looks after the health of men
5. Charakilongmei: The god who keeps peace and ward off disturbance on earth.
6. Koklou: The Peipou, the owner of the office of god's court
7. Karangong: The god who is a teaser of unruly and misbehaved persons particularly youth. Healer of man suffering from dizziness.
8. Dimei: The deity who could not hatch and remains under the earth.

The abodes of the divine brothers are as follows:

i). Ragwang (Na-Ragwang) took residence at Mt. Koubru

ii). Bisnu's abode is at holy cave of Bhuvan Hills

iii). Napsinmei's abode is at the peak of Napsinmei Hill, Ganglon Namthan in the old Cachar Road

iv). Chonchai resides at the Mt. Kasokbut, Taosang Khullen village in Tamenglong district v). Charakilongmei lives at the mountain peak of Bena village (Thonglang) at the western spur of Mt. Koubru

vi). Koklou resides at the peak over the Pongringlong village in the Koubru-Laimatol range

vii). Karangong is believed to reside at Puching (Kheba Ching) in Tamenglong district.

viii). Dimei, the brother who did not hatch remains in the water.

There are gods and deities in-charge of wind, fire, animals, paddy, thunder, earthquake who are being worshipped in this sacrifice. In an exceptional case of Chingmeirong village, the Raangpatmei ceremony is performed in the second day of the Gaan Ngai festival. In the village of Chingkham, this sacrifice is performed at the end of the Rih Ngai destival. However, in lower Rongmei villages of Tamenglong district and Manipur valley areas, it is performed at the end of the Gaan Ngai festival.

After the performance of the Raren loumei, the elders and the priest will proceed to the village council (Pei) and performed the Bukaomei ceremony (calling of souls) by offering a fowl to Tingkao Ragwang, the Supreme God. They will offer holy wine and the meat of the fowl after being cooked will be distributed in pieces to every household in the village. This marks formally the end of the Gaan Ngai festival.

(Chaoba Kamson, Chakan Gaan Ngai: The living religious and cultural festival, 2012, Imphal, pp. 57-58; See also Lanbilung Gonmei, Gods and Goddesses of the Zeliangrong Community in Socio-Cultural and Spiritual Traditions of Zeliangrong, edited by Chaoba Kamson, Heritage Foundation, Guwahati, 2011)

Puan nimmei

At the end of Gaan Ngai, there are exchange of gifts between the boys and girls in the respective dormitories. The leaders of the dormitories present gifts to the owner of the boys' and girls' dormitory. These gifts are given in forms of necklace, earrings, and bangles as the token cost of the damage done to the utensils and other tools of the dormitory owners. These gifts are also exchanged among the boys and girls.

In present times, instead of the gifts, money was given by the members of the dormitory to the owner of the dormitory. It is a very solemn presentation of the monetary gifts preceded by respectful request for forgiveness of the erring members of the dormitory for the damage done to the owner of the dormitory. Earlier, the members of the dormitory present gifts to the elders during the performance of Longkumei. They also present the gifts to the elders on the occasion of Raangpatmei. This isknown as Raangpat puan as both the dormitories, Khangchu and Luchu will hand over puan meaning money as an exchange of boys and girls, to the elders of the village council.

The Gaan Ngai has covered several activities of the Zeliangrong people, religious, cultural, customary, physical sports, maintenance of discipline among the people.

The worship to Tingkao Ragwang to protect men from death or danger and provide longevity, welfare and prosperity is the most important objective of the Gaan Ngai festival. The people worship all the gods and deities of the Zeliangrong pantheon. They worship God for plentiful harvest. They also bid farewell to the departed souls.

The Gaan Ngai festival sustains the Zeliangrong culture. The singing competition in the dormitories, beating of the drums and playing of musical instruments like Raa jaimei, performance of dance of different patterns and singing of village guarding songs are unique cultural aspects of the Gaan Ngai festival.

Gaan Ngai also strengthens the traditional social institutions. They admit new members to the dormitories; supervise the entry of young adolescence (both boys and girls) to dormitories; promotion of members of the dormitory to other higher institutions of Gaanchang and Baanja. During the Gaan Ngai nely weded women are formally admitted to the women institution (Mathenmei).

The Gaan Ngai also carried out games and sports like long jump, stone throwing, wrestling and spear throwing.

The Gaan enforces discipline in the behavior of boys and girls. The dormitory leaders enforce strict control by issue of advice known as Thing-ngun kadimei (teaching by whip).

Lastly, the community life and social interaction organized through the dormitories both boys and girls controlled by leaders divided by age grade hierarchy promotes unity, love, brotherhood among the community particularly the youth. The Zeliangrong society and culture are sustained by these festivals in the performance of which the whole village starting from the village council, youth dormitories, women institutions, offices of the elders participate.

6

Gaan Ngai in an Urban Setting

The reality of a festival is seen when it is performed in the village and at the household level. The Gaan Ngai is a living and popular festival. It is proposed to document and confirm the institutions of the villages which were in existence for the conduct of the festival. For an empirical study it is proposed to study the Gaan Ngai festival at a Zeliangrong village in Manipur valley. The name of the village is called Majorkhul. There are valid reasons for the choice of this village for my study. Majorkhul is a village inhabited by Rongmei speakers of the Zeliangrong community. The community leaders of the village have a fairly an intimate communication with all sections of the tribal community and non tribal communities. Therefore it is a fairly exposed village and one can easily observe the influences of other communities on the performance of Gaan Ngai festival. Majorkhul is a very old village which was established during the pre colonial days when Major Shamu Singh of the Manipur Army granted the settlement of this village for a group of Rongmei settlers. The inhabitants of this village have a strong attachment to their village and religion. They had come into conflicts with the British colonial authorities while they persue the indigenous religion and perform their annual festivals. They had survived in this struggle and are very proud of belonging to this village. The author, herself belongs to this village and knows the elders, youths and community leaders of the village. It is easier for her to conduct the investigation on the social, religious and cultural aspects of the Gaan Ngai festival in this village. Luckily our assumption is found to be correct. Therefore, two tools of research were applied; collecting information through verbal interview with the elders, leaders and participants of the festival and secondary information collected from the written publications about the village, village dormitory known as Khangchu. Participant observer method was adopted in reconstructing the performance of Gaan Ngai festival.

Majorkhul is a Naga locality in the urban area of Imphal town. Majorkhul is a "village" in the context of social and cultural purposes. The community is organized socially and culturally through the village. Other functions of the urban administration are maintained by the Government agencies like Police, Revenue, PWD department and Imphal Municipal Council. A distinctive feature of Majorkhul which impresses an observer is the maintenance of cultural including social and religious features of a traditional Naga village. The people of Majorkhul are proud of their culture, religion and social life. They are also ready to accept the changes brought about by modernity. Majorkhul is a small locality of 85 households surrounded by several urban localities like the Government offices of PWD, Manipur Assembly Guest House and other residences of the ministers and commercial establishments run by non Nagas. Majorkhul male dormitory published a hand out entitled, "Khangchu". This hand out gives the detail of the organization and function of various festivals in the village. The village performs seven festivals at present as noted below:

1. Gaan Ngai – January/ Wakching or Pous 13
2. Rih Ngai – February
3. Ganthan Luithan Bapmei – March
4. Nanu Ngai – March
5. Napkao + Ginki Ngai – April
6. Gudui + Maleng Ngai – May

   (Tun Ngai and Ten Ngai were abolished)
7. Pukphat Ngai – September

   (There is no Dongjao Ngai or Chakak Ngai)

Socially the male members of the community are divided into several grades on the basis of age. The male members of a Zeliangrong village are divided into six grades namely, the Banza, the Gaanchang and four grades of the dormitory which are further divided on the basis of age; they are Khangbon, Gaanpi Kaijibmei, Gaanpi Phongchakmei and Ganna (Shingkhangloi). At the time of my survey, the following elders are the Banza of the village.

1. Abui Kamei, Khullakpu
2. Gaijenlung Palmei, Luplakpu
3. Gaithaochung Golmei, Khunpu
4. R. Tampikhon, Mantri
5. G. Thomas, Meitei Lampu

The following are the four Gaanchangs of the village

1. Abuina Golmei, Khangchupou (owner of the boys' dormitory)
2. A. Pourongai Golmei, Luchupou (owner of the girls' dormitory)
3. S. Khangmeidun Kamei
4. Gaikompu Phaomei

The Banzas and the Gaanchangs are members of the Village Council (Pei).

The male dormitory known as Khangchu has four grades of membership.

1. Khangbon
2. Gaanpi Kaijibmei
3. Gaanpi Phongchakmei
4. Singkhangloi

Currently Majorkhul Khangchu has got the following members according to their seniority. Khangbon:

1. Meijinlung Kamson
2. Monthajei Kamei
3. Gangmumei Kamei
4. Gaiguplung Gangmei.

Gaanpi Kaijibmei has 22 members; Gaanpi Phongchakmei has 20 members and Shingkhangloi has 145 members.

The girls' dormitory known as Luchu has 95 members.

The Gaan Ngai festival is managed by the dormitories under the supervision of the village council. The coming of the Gaan Ngai festival is observed as per the following processes. The announcement of the Gaan Ngai is made by the Gaanshanmei, blowing of the horn of mithun or cattle. In Majorkhul the announcement of the Gaan Ngai is made through the shouting of the Napui lengtho which means the villagers are to prepare rice beer by drying paddy from the granaries and making of Napok (sprouted paddy) for the preparation of rice beer. During the Gaan Ngai of this year, the elder of Majorkhul who announced the Napui lengtho was Gaithaochung Golmei on 26th December 2011. Gaithochung Golmei holds the office of Khunpu and is also a priest (Taku). With the announcement of this news the youth of the boys' dormitory will prepare the jumping ground of the village, Danshanpung for the long jump competition. The boys' dormitory also considered the observation of Gaan Ngai after the announcement of this message. They will announce the rate of subscription of the members of the dormitory known as Tamcha. They will also search for suitable animals either cattle or pig for community feast. The youth also collect a kind of bamboo known as "Gu" which is needed for head dress and production of fire. The dormitory will inspect the position of the material for the production of new fire. They will also enquire the selection of leaders of the village for upward promotion, choice of youth for selection of "Phak" kings and queens, farewell dance for the dead and for the girls going to be married. Before the commencement of the festival, the elders will announce for preparation of rice beer.

On the eve of the Gaan Ngai in Majorkhul, I observed the following. The elders sent out a message that every household should prepare eatables either animal, birds or vegetables. On the occasion of this festival, the village council distributed Rs. 1100/- for every household to meet the expenditure. An amount of Rs. 100/- was deducted from every household to meet the cost of the religious sacrifice known as Raren loumei to be performed on the day of Raangpatmei. Secondly, the eve of Gaan Ngai falls on 6th January 2012. It coincides with the occasion of community feast peformed by women folk of the village, Mathenmei as they bid farewell to two leaders of the womenfolk who are going to be promoted to that of Kengjapui (old women). The two leaders are Leipaklei Golmei and Achapi Golmei. The elders in-charge of controlling the women folk who are known as Lakpui munsinmei (those who control the speech of women) are Gaithaochung Golmei and R. Tampikhon who are the members of the village council. On this day, the young wives who are married to the young husbands of the village in the previous year are given ceremonial admission known as Pothamei (presenting of gifts). The function was held in the office of Mathenmei. They killed a pig to entertain the two leaders who are being promoted to Kengjapui. The Mathenmei give presents to the two leaders. It was announced by the Lakpui munsinmei that the farewell dance in honour of the two ladies would be held after the Gaan Ngai festival. A description of this dance is given at the end of this chapter with photo illustration.

The members of the dormitory attended their dormitory with the submision of their Gaan Ngai subscription (Tamcha) at the rate of Rs. 205/- for Khangbon, Rs. 155/- for Gaanpi and Rs. 105/- for Shingkhangloi and Rs. 85/- for girls. This day is popularly known as day of Thingtinmei (collection of firewood). The members of the dormitory proceeded towards the northern gate and brought pieces of firewood to the dormitory. It was a token submission of firewood to a dormitory. When the members of the dormitory were gathered, wife of the owner of the male dormitory would present rice beer and chutney to the gathering. The elders of the dormitory will inspected the state of preparedness of the Gaan Ngai festival which was being started on the next day.

Ngai Gangmei

Ngai Gangmei means the advent of the festival. It is a first day and it falls on 7th January, 2012.

Danjaomei: The danjaomei rite which was omen learning rite was performed at the dawn (before the day break). The village elders gathered at the northern abode of the village deity known as the 'Kaipi bambu bam' and performed the said rite. Gaithaochung Golmei was the priest who performed the Danjaomei rite. He was accompanied by elders like Khangmeidun, Gaikompu, Thomas, Abuina, Meijinlung, Monthajei, Gaiguplung, Chandrasing and Sangpuna. The rite was preceded by the offer of 'Joupan keimei', offer of holy wine to the 3 deities of the village. The first one was to Ragwang or Tingkao Ragwang, the Supreme God, the second was village deities namely, Kaipi Bambu and Kaiba Bambu of northern and southern side and the third was to the ancestors of the village. The priest laid down a banana leaf and threw three pairs of ginger pieces to above deities and he learned the omen by seeing the position of the gingers. The priest announced that the omen was good and it was indicative of prosperity of the village. (See the photo). Then the village elders headed by the priest proceeded to the southern abode of the deity, Kaiba Bambu. The priest performed the worship and returned to the male dormitory led by other elders.

Gakpai jaomei (Interpreting the spleen of the pig): At the boys' dormitory, there was a sacrifice of a boar to the Tingkao Ragwang (Ragwang), the village deities and ancestors of the village. The priest, Gaithaochung Golmei offered holy wine to the deities. Then the boar was brought to the worshipping place and the priest gave blessings to those youths who succeded in catching the animal. A youth named Poujanglin killed the boar with the iron hammer. Poujanglin cut open the abdomen of the animal and removed the spleen. The spleen was washed out and laid down over a plaintain leaf in a winnowing basket. The elders of the village led by the priest followed by Tampikhon, Gaikompu, Meijinlung, Khangmeidun, etc. interpreted the size, shape of the spleen and unanimously declared that it was a good omen for the village. The people were happy. The holy wine was again offered. The boar after being cleaned off his hairs by burning was smeared with turmeric and grasses put into the ears was cut into several pieces according to the anatomy of the animal. Sanjee Kamei under the direction of the head of the dormitory, Meijinling Kamson cut the animal. This was a very painstaking and intricate process known as 'Jan phakmei'. The limbs of the boar starting from the legs, breast bones, neck bones, flesh of the back, pieces of fats, flesh of the inside back, buttock, abdominal flesh were cut out for presentation to the respective functionaries. The distribution of the pieces of the meat is also called 'Saram lathaomei'. The following pieces of the meat were distributed to the respective elders and functionaries of the dormitory. Two hind legs, two front legs, two breast bones, two leg bones were distributed to the functionaries of the dormitory.

1. Meijinlung Kamson – Hind leg
2. Monthajei Kamei – Hind leg
3. Gangmumei Kamei – Front leg
4. Gaigupling Gangmei – Front leg
5. Chandrasing – Kaloudong
6. Gangangpu – Kaloudong
7. Pantigangpu Golmei – Flesh of the lower leg
8. Sangpuna – Kaphulou – Flesh of the lower leg

Thangka keimei consisting of a piece of meat and live charcoal was offered to God. The dormitory also the gave following parts of the boar to the wife of the owner of the dormitory (Kaipei saram). Piece of liver, piece of heart, abdominal meat, piece of fats, piece of rib, flesh of lower leg, breast bone, piece of lungs, flesh of outer back and flesh of inner back and buttock. The members of Banza and Gaanchang were given flesh with genital and pieces of fats. Pieces of meat known as 'janphob' were distribted for young boys who would be admitted to the dormitory next year. The meat was also given to the girls' dormitory for their feasting.

The Gaan Ngai feast: Jeigan Tumei

The feast of the Gaan Ngai started with the invocation of Almighty God by the rhythmic shouting of ho-hoing known as Naplao Hoi (Hoi for the feasting). The community feast of Majorkhul dormitory consisted of "Jeigan Tumei" which meant "eating of the curry of the insides of the animal cooked with the blood". Jeigan Tumei was the affirmation in the strength, fraternity and victory of the village. It was followed by the normal meals. Khangchupei, the wife of the owner of the dormitory presented a bowl of vegetable chutney and rice beer to the community. The members of the dormitory presented a meal (consisting of rice and curry) to the Khangchupei (owner of the dormitory) and to the Luchupou, the owner of the girls' dormitory. They also distributed plates of meals to those who were absent in the festival.

Hoigammei (Hoi procession)

Hoigammei was the main ceremonial procession of the festival marching across the village in full traditional attire. Every elder, members of the male dormitory including Khangbon, Gaanpi and Shingkhangloi participated in this procession. They put on their best dresses wearing the "Phei ngao" and holding the spears. The procession started from the courtyard of the dormitory. The Khangchupei presented a vegetable chutney, rice beer and tea to the community. The youth of the dormitory distributed a head dress made of Goo bamboo known as Pikam to all the elders and senior members of the dormitory. The procession started with the ho-hoing followed by beating of the drum, cymbals and gong. They proceeded to the northern gate by shouting "Changtat hoi" (marching hoi) and performed "Hoikadingmei" at the northern gate. It was a very beautiful scene to see the hoi procession across the village. From the northern gate they proceeded to the south eastern gate at the eastern side of the village. They again proceeded to the southern gate where they performed "Hoikadingmei". Then they proceeded to the village jumping ground known as "Danshanpung" where they did Hoikadingmei again. There were competitions of long jump and stone throwing.

The people of the village came out to see these competitions. The stone throwing was inaugurated by Abuina Golmei, Khangchupou, owner of the male dormitory. There was also a shot put competition. Many boys of the village participated. After the shot put competition, the long jump was inaugurated by Gaikompu Phaomei, a Gaanchang of the village. Many youth again participated in the competition. Kinthuilung Phaomei was the winner in the shot put competition and Lansingam Kamei in the long jump. At the end of the competition, the dormitory leaders announced the names of the winners. It was followed by the "Mailapmei", al ceremonial production of new fire by the method of friction of bamboo pieces and dry soft woods. After the production of sacred new fire, it was distributed to every household of the village. The youths went back to their dormitory. The elders in group visited every household reminding that members of the household should not create any tension or quarrel on the occasion of Gaan Ngai and whoever did that was warned to be penalized by the village council.

Napkao in individual households

The community aspect of Gaan Ngai has been described. Every household particularly led by the wives of the householders participated in the festival by offering a ceremony of 'Napkaomei' (calling of the goddess of paddy). This ceremony in every household made the participation of the women folk possible. After offering of a fowl, it was cooked and the lady of the hose performed 'Napchanmei' ceremony by offering pieces of liver, rice, ginger and rice beer to the deities presiding over the family's hearth, Kambuipui, Charaipui and Kairao.

After the hoigammei procession was over, boys and girls participated in a joint dinner where each one of them brought meals for partaking. After this the boys and girls performed joint singing in their respective dormitories.

Some youths went out to go around the village by singing the village guarding songs (Kairong lonlu) throughout the night. Thus ended the Ngai gangmei day of the Gaan Ngai festival at Majorkhul on 7th January 2012.

Tamchan and Tuna-Gaan Ngai

The second day of Gaan Ngai is normally called 'Ngai dai' the main festival. It consists of a number of occasions namely the Tamchan Ngai; farewell dances to Khangbon being promoted to Gaanchang known as 'Khangbon kadimei'; Thei kadimei, farewell dance to the death and farewell dance to the girl to be married. Because of involvement of the boys and girls in these functions, this day of the Gaan Ngai is also called Tuna-Gaan Ngai (the festival of boys and girls). On this day in Majorkhul there is the Tamchan tingmik, day of Tamchan and Tuna-Gaan Ngai. On this day the members of the dormitory of the grade of Gaanpi and shingkhangloi gave a subscription (Tamcha) to the dormitory. Tamcha was giving of subscription in kind given to the dormitory. The girl also gave Tuna Tamcha, girl subscription to the girls' dormitory. Nowadays the payment of Tamcha was substituted by monetary payment. This year the Khangbon, Gaanpi, Shingkhangloi and Tuna (girls) paid monetrary subscription in lieu of Tamcha. Tamcha had become to mean subscription of the members of the dormitory.

There was no Tamchan Laam (dances preformed in the offices of Banza kaibang, Gaanchang kaibang and Kengjapui kaibang). The performance of Tamchan Laam was discontinued long ago. However Majorkhul dormitory continued to perform the farewell dances in honour of Khangbon (Khangbon kadimei), the (Theikadimei) and girls to be married (Tuna kadimei). The Majorkhul dormitory used to perform the Khangbon kadimei dances whenever there were promotions of Khangbon to Gaanchang. In 2012, there was no Khangbon kadimei as there was no promotion of any Khangbon to the post of Gaanchang. It may be mentioned that in the past year, 2011 two heads of the male dormitory, S. Khangmeidun Kamei and Gaikompu Phaomei who were seniormost Khangbons were promoted to the post of Gaanchang. Both of them performed the Khangbon kadimei in a grand scale. Each one of them gave a farewell feast by entertaining the whole community of Majorkhul and their relatives outside the village on separate days. On the Tuna-Gaan Ngai day, both Khangemidun and Gaikompu were given farewell dances by the members of the Majorkhul dormitories. Khangemidun Kamei presented an amount of Rs. 26,000/- as 'shon', gift for blessing to the dancing members of the village dormitory. Gaikompu Phaomei also presented an almost similar amount as the 'shon'. The Khangbon kadimei dances are beautiful, varied and colourful. The boys and girls were dressed in the dancing costumes and performed the dances in the courtyard of the two khangbons. The artistic beauty of the Zeliangrong dances is retained through this beautiful kadimei dances.

This year there was an unfortunate death of Johnnybond Golmei, son of Abuina Golmei, the Khangchupou of the village. Johnnybond passed away of heart attack. His parents requested the authority of the boys' dormitory that the boys' dormitory might not perform Theikadimei (farewell to the deal) dance in honour of their departed son. Instead they informed the dormitory that they would present in terms of utensils like pots, pans, pressure cooker, etc. and other eatables to the dormitory. In fact the parents gave 'thei tamcha' (subscription of the dead) to the dormitory. Payment of Tamcha was a special presentation as tamcha was collected by dormitory from each member. The authorities of the dormitory accepted the presentation of the gifts in honour of Johnnybond. So a solemn function was held at the courtyard of the dormitory where the parents presented the said item of gifts to the dormitory. There were women guests who were invited to the function. On behalf of the male dormitory, the Khangbon kasung (head of the Khangbon), Meijinlung Kamson acknowledged the receipt of the gifts and gave a condolence speech. After this tamcha presentation ceremony, there were no other items of festival in Majorkhul this year. The second day passed off without much festivity.

Longruimei (hill trekking) and Phakgwang Laam

The third day of the festival was called longruimei or longkumei (hill trekking). It fell on the 9th January 2012. In the past longruimei was organized in a big way. Both male and female membes of the dormitories went out to see the surrounding mountains near their village. They choose two boys and two girls as kings and queens of 'Phak', a type of grass. They were known as Phakgwangs. They would bring 'Gaktingtam', chutney pounded with pork, ginger and chillies and made into balls, would be distributed to the elders and members of the dormitories for eating. The rice beer was also offered to the members. Only the girls would perform dance at the selected hill range. Then they returned to the village and performed dances in honour of the four kings and queens. This was known as Phakgwang Laam, the dance of Phak kings and Phak queens.

Majorkhul is an urban area; there is no hill nearby and it is not convenient to go out in trekking in distant hills. Therefore the Majorkhul dormitory chose the children park of the village where longruimei (hill trekking) was observed in a token form. Unfortunately this year, on the day of Longruimei there was a heavy downpour throughout the day. It was not possible to go out to the children park for the observation of the hill trekking. Therefore the elders decided to shift the place of Longruimei at the abode of the village deity, Bambu at the northern gate of the village. Fortunately the abode of the Bambu was covered by a pandal like building which was roofed properly to give shelter from the heavy rains. The boys and girls proceeded to the abode of the Bambu and performed the longruimei ceremony. The youths of the dormitory presented money (paunimmei) to the elders. The boys and girls dormitories presented Gaktingtam (pork chutney), rice beer and tea to all the members. The village priest offered holy wine to the God, deities of the village and ancestors. The girls performed a dance inside the pandal like house building. As stated earlier on this day only the dance was to perform dance. But in Majorkhul as per the request of the girls the boys also participated in the dance.

The Phakgwang Laam was to be performed in honour of four boys and four girls. The four boys were Shyam Kamei, Lanshinlung Golmei, Johnny Gangmei and Khanglujei Golmei. The girls were Gaisinlu Phaomei, Tampuina Longmei, Jenny Palmei and Pougang Golmei. It was proposed that the Phakgwang Laam would be performed at the courtyard of girls' dormitoru (Luchu) in honour of the Luchupou, owner of the girls' dormitory, A. Pourongai Golmei who was sick for sometime. The youth of the dormitory repaired the courtyard of the girls' dormitory. Unfortunately due to heavy rains, the idea of performing dance at the courtyard of girls' dormitory was given up. It had become a dilemma for the members of the dormitory to perform dance or not. Then it was ultimately decided that the Phakgwang laam would be performed inside the community hall of the village. The community hall was a high wall building and could accommodate 500 spectators. Since it was becoming dark the problem of electricity also came up whether there would be sufficient light for the dancing boys and girls. Despite the deficiencies the Phakgwang Laam was performed in the community hall while the torrential rains were pouring down.

The eight kings and queens of Phak contributed money to the dormitory to arrange tea and snacks. It was a unique experience because nobody had experienced the performance of the festival dances in a community hall. Each of the Phakgwang was presented two dances accompanied by songs. The elders and members of the dormitory participated in singing and beating the drums. The dances which were performed in the festivals were known as Chapa (Tapa) Laam. There were also nearly 40 Chapa (Tapa) songs. But in Majorkhul they repeated six songs were sing on this day. Sang only 7 Chapa songs on the occasion of Phakgwang Laam. The elders and the leaders of the dormitory faced great inconveniences in singing following the dancing boys and girls. The dance started around 4.30 p.m and ended at around 11 p.m. Each of the Phakgwangs gave a gift of Rs. 1000/- as shon to the dormitory. This amount was fixed by the village authority. Further they prohibited entertainment of guests in their respective homes by killing four footed animals. The Longruimei followed by the Phakgwang Laam ended amidst the dancing in the rains at the community hall. However the dancers proceeded to the boys' dormitory and girls' dormitory to perform the last dances.

Napchanmei

In Majorkhul, Napchanmei ceremony marked the fourth day or the closing day of the Gaan Ngai festival. Napchanmei means worship of goddess of paddy and wealth by performing Napkaomei ritual. Napkaomei is calling of the goddess of paddy. In the morning of this day, there was a gathering of members of the two dormitories and presented the gift amounts to the girls' dormitory for the performance of the napchanmei. The dormitories also presented money gifts to the Banza and Gaanchang elders who participated in the singing of songs in the previous night, Phakgwang Laam. The wastages of food and eatables were to be restored with the blessing of the goddess of paddy. The main occasion of the worship of Napkaomei was held in the boys' dormitory. The ceremony consisted of offering of a handsome fowl followed by a sacrifice of a pig. The Napkaomei ceremony at the boys' dormitory was performed by the priest Gaithaochung

Golmei, Banza and Khunpu assisted by Gaikompu Phaomei, a Gaanchang. A fowl with his leg tied to the tail of the pig was offered to God asking for blessings and offer of thanksgiving. After chanting of the hymns the cock was strangulated and an omen was read at the position of its legs. The holy wine was offered to the God, village deities and ancestors. Then the pig was sacrificed, its spleen was cut open and it was interpreted to see the omen. The priest and the elders announced that the position of the legs of the fowl and the spleen indicated that there would be prosperity and happiness in the village.

There was a similar ceremony of Napkaomei in the girls' dormitory. The two Tunamunsinmei (incharge of girls) namely, Chandrasing Golmei and Sangpuna Phaomei managed the feast at the girls' dormitory. The members of the dormitory prepared the meat for a community feast. All the members of the dormitory were gathered and participated in this joint community work cutting meat and cooking pork and cooking rice. In the individual houses, the worship of the goddess of paddy and wealth was performed by performance of Napkaomei ritual. The wives of the household cooked the meat of the fowl and pieces of its liver, cooked rice, wine and ginger were offered to the deities presiding over the hearth.

Napchanmei was marked by a grand feast at the boys' dormitory. The elders of the village, the leaders of the dormitory and younger members of the dormitory and other children of the village were invited to attend the feast. The feast was preceded by the invocation of supreme God by shouting of Naplao Hoi accompanied by beating of drums, cymbals and gongs. The leaders of the dormitory sent out meals to the respective Khangchupei, (wife of the dormitory owner), Luchupei (wife of the owner of the girls' dormitory) and the absentee members of the dormitory. They also presented meals to the families living around the neighbourhood of the dormitory. The community feast on 10th January 2012 was a successful dinner and everybody was cheerful. After the feast at the boys' dormitory, elders were invited to the girls' dormitory to partake their dinner. The girls' dormitory also presented meals to the boys' dormitory. They also distributed meals to those girls who could not come. After the community feast both at the boys and girls dormitory was over, youth of the boys' dormitory sang a kind of mocking song known as Napsin Gansinlaomei which was usually appreciated by all members of the dormitory. The dinner was followed by a singing competition between the boys and girls at the girls' dormitory. Other boys who did not participate in the singing competition went out singing the village guarding song across the village. Thus ended the Napchanmei day of the Gaan Ngai festival of 2012.

Raangpatmei

Raangpatmei is not part of the Gaan Ngai festival. It was an offer of sacrifices to the God and deities of the Zeliangrong community. Raagpatmei literally means going beyond the village gate. It was performed at the end of the Gaan Ngai festival. The God and deities were worshipped and propitiated as it is believed that they came to attend the Gaan Ngai festival. The main function of the Raangpatmei was the performance of the sacrifice of Raren loumei (worshipping of all gods.and deities). The Raangpat ceremony was carried out by the elders of the village council and not by the members of the dormitory. The Raangpatmei ceremony was performed on 11th January 2012 at the northern gate of the village. The village council collected an amount of Rs. 100/- from every household to meet the expenses of the Raren loumei ceremony for purchasing cocks, eggs, ginger and plaintain leaves. It was an important village worship day. The elders announced Neihmei (genna) for the village. The entry of outsiders into the village was not allowed but it was nowadays liberalized. It was a sacrifice in which every household and individual was involved in worshipping the gods and deities of the Zeliangrong community.

Raren loumei

Raren loumei was the offer of sacrifices to all deities of the Zeliangrong community which were also worshipped by Majorkhul village. The chief priest who offeref the sacrifices of cocks and eggs was Gaithaochung Golmei who performed all the religious ceremonies of the Gaan Ngai festival. He was assisted by the village elders who had attained the status of Banza and Gaanchang. The elders who participated in this sacrifice were R. Tampikhon, Thomas Golmei, Abuina Golmei, Khangmeidun Kamei and Gaikompu Phaomei. The author got the opportunity of interviewing these elders to find out names of the deities in which Raren loumei was performed. Abuina Golmei, the Gaanchang and Khangchupou of the dormitory read out from a document the names of the deities being worshipped on that day. Gaithochung Golmei and Gaikompu Phaomei explained the religious belief of the Zeliangrong people being worshipped in the village. Gaithaochung said that the village worships the seven brother gods of Ragwang and other deities which are worshipped in the nearby hills and villages. Therefore the gods worshipped by Meities, Hindus are being also worshipped by the village. The following are the 29 deities who are worshiped on the occasion of Raren loumei.

Sl.	*Name of deities*	*Item of offering*
1.	Ragwang	Cock, ginger, wine
2.	Bisnu	-do-
3.	Napsinmei	-do-
4.	Chonchai	Cock, ginger, water
5.	Karangong	Cock, ginger, wine
6.	Charakilongmei	-do-
7.	Kokloumei	-do-

(These seven deities are known as seven brother of the God, Ragwang)

8. Karagang	Cock, ginger, wine
9. Taijang	-do-
10. Tairong	-do-
11. Yangoi Ningthou	-do-
12. Tingthoungampu	-do-
13. Mahadev	-do-
14. Langol Ningthou	-do-
15. Pakhangpu	-do-
16. Kheba Ningthou	-do-
17. Kangpokpi	-do-
18. Yumjao Lairemma	-do-
19. Pukhri Daimei	-do-
20. Taoring	-do-
21. Maigang (God of fire)	egg
22. Pongang (God of wind)	egg
23. Banglagwang (God of earthquake)	egg
24. Tingbugang (God of white ants)	egg
25. Champei (God of animals)	egg
26. Dimei (one who cannot hatch)	egg
27. Kunmei (A stationary spirit of the village)egg	
28. Parȧ (evil spirit)	fowl cut into two halves
29. Kali	pigeon

And a hen will be offered as a scapegoat of the village community.

The cock offered to Ragwang was given to the priest after cleansing of its feathers. The cocks from item no. 2 to 20 were cooked and eaten by the elders who joined the ceremony and the children. The eggs from item no. 21 to 27 are just broken by way of offering to the deities. After the sacrifices were over, village elder in a special message informed the villagers to worship at the sacrifice. Several women folk came out to worship the deities.

On the day of Raangpatmei, the village dormitory offered a monetary gift to the elders. The sacrifice was followed by the feast of the cooked chicken. The elders and children brought rice and each one of them was given chicken meat. At the end of the feasting, a Gaanchang named Thomas Golmei was announced to be promoted to the post of Banza. This was concluded by shouting of Hoi.

The elders procede to the Peikai, office of the village council. In the courtyard of the peikai, the village priest performed the ceremony of Bukaomei (calling of souls). A cock would be sacrificed to the Supreme God, Tingkao Ragwang so that the people in the village would have long life, good health and prosperity. It was followed by offering of holy wine to the God and deities. The elders of the village attended the ceremony. While the cock was being cooked, the elders of the village proceeded to the house of Thomas Golmei affirming his promotion as a Banza. After the chicken was cooked the pieces of the meat was distributed to all the households of the village informing them that they had offered sacrificed to the Supreme God.

Paun Nimmei

Next day the members of the dormitory offered monetary gifts known as Paun Nimmei to the owners of the dormitories. In the morning of 12th January the elders and leaders of the boys' dormitory presented the paun (gift) to the Khangchupou and Khangchupei (owner and wife of the dormitory). Khangchupou was Abuina Golmei and Khangchupei was Chindenpi Golmei. The couple was hospitable towards the dormitory. The family offered tea and snacks to the members of the dormitory. They also accepted monetary gifts presented to them. The girls' dormitory also presented paun to the Luchupou and Luchupei (owner and wife of the girls' dormitory). The delegation of the girls' dormitory consisted of both village elders, members of the dormitories including the two Tunamunsinmei. The paun in form of monetary gifts was presented to Luchupou and Luchupei who accepted the paun. A. Pourongai Golmei was the Luchupou and Lujailu Golmei was the Luchupei. During the exchange of gifts the couple became emotional due to the long illness of Luchupou. Everybody wished the Luchupou for quick recovery and many years of service and guidance to the village and the dormitory. Practically the Gaan Ngai festival 2012 had thus come to an end.

Laakpui kadimei

There was an additional special dance of the married women this year. As noted earlier on the eve of Gaan Ngai festival, women folk of Majorkhul Mathenmei organized a special lunch in honour of two leaders namely Leipaklei Golmei and Achapi Golmei who were promoted to the post of Kengjapui. Gifts were presented to them. Two leaders of Mathenmei known as Laakpui munsinmei namely Gaithaochung Golmei and R. Tampikhon were given farewell by the Mathenmei. As the women folk required longer time for learning of dancing it was decided that the farewell dances for the two ladies would be held on 15th January 2012. The women dancers consisted of nearly 120 persons. Two male elders namely R. Tampikhon and Gaikompu Phaomei were the leaders of the dancing group. The dances were really well performed with beauty, colour and dignity. Most of the women folk of Majorkhul turned out to be good dancers. The two dances were observed by large number of people including non Naga communities. The women folk really enjoyed this kadimei laam. The two ladies for whom the farewell dances were performed presented monetary gifts to the Mathenmei group. Leipaklei Golmei gave Rs. 20,111/- and Achapi Golmei gave Rs. 41,011/- as shon to the Mathenmei. Thus the Gaan Ngai festival which consisted of several feasts, dances and ceremonies came to an end.

Danjaomei (omen taking by ginger) before day break by Gaithaochung Golmei on 7th January 2012

Hoigammei (Hoi procession) at Majorkhul

Mailapmei (Making of the new fire) by youth of Majorkhul

Tamcha ponmei ceremony in honour of late Poulen Golmei (Johnnybond) at the dormitory

Phakgwang felicitation dance in honour of 4 boys and 4 girls

Girls dancing at Longruimei (hill trekking)

Phakgwang dance

The girls of Phakgwang Laam

Napchanmei: Napkaomei (calling the goddess of paddy) by priest Gaithaochung Golmei

Rangpatmei: Raren loumei (sacrifice to all deities of Zeliangrong pantheon)

Farewell dance in honour of Leipaklei Golmei and Achaapi Golmei by Mathenmei

Puanimmei - Presentation of gifts to Luchupou, A.P. Golmei, owner of the girls' dormitory

Gifts presented to Leipaklei Golmei and Achapi Golmei

7

Towards Modernity

The Zeliangrong people came into slow contact with the foreigners and neighbours mostly through trade and commerce. They came into contact with the Naga tribes of Mao, Maram, Poumai and Thangal in north Manipur. They had close social and trading connection with the Angami tribe. They traded with the Kachari tribes under whose ruler some of them were subjects. Among the foreigners their contact with the Meiteis was a combination of hostile relation due to frequent raids and counters raids and followed with trade contacts. In the 19th century they came into contact with the Meitei, Kachari and Angami traders. The British explorers came to know of Zeliangrong tribes in early 19th century. During the first Anglo-Burmese War Lt. R.B. Pemberton visited the Zeliangrong villages in western Manipur. He visited the villages of Oinamlong, Nungba, Mongjaron Khunou and Khoupum. He described the Nagas (which mean the Zeliangrong people) as a fine people. The Treaty of 1833 concluded between Manipur and East India Company provided a provision for the protection of trading rights of the Nagas in the markets of Cachar. The Zeliangrong Nagas were to construct the Cachar road between Silchar and Bishenpur under the British supervision free of cost. The Cachar road was constructed by Zeliangrong labour and the Manipuri kings imposed strict administration in the villages living in and around the Cachar road. The Manipuri kings appreciated the dances of the Zeliangrong Nagas. Even the British officers took note of the festivals and dances of the Zeliangrong Nagas. In course of time it had become a fashion for a Manipur Government to present the dances of the Zeliangrong Nagas whenever British dignitaries visited capital of Manipur. During the fateful visit of Chief Commissioner of Assam, Quinton on 23rd March 1891, the Manipur Durbar proposed to present Kabui (Rongmei) Naga dance at the Residency of the Political Agent where the Chief Commissioner and his party were put up. The dance was cancelled due to the tension between the kingdom of Manipur and Chief Commissioner of Assam. Mrs. Ethel Grimwood, the unfortunate wife of Political Agent Grimwood in her book, "My Three Years in Manipur" mentioned the employment of Zeliangrong Nagas in the service of the British Political Agency. She mentioned her meeting with a Naga Band Master belonging to this community who played beautiful English music at the Gurkha Rifles garrison at Langthabal. The modern instrumental music was appreciated both by the Maharaja of Manipur and the British Political Agent. Maipak, the first Christian convert of the community was a musician. He was employed by the Raja Churachand Singh as a Band Master of the Manipur State Police. The Raja was fond of Maipak before the latter's conversion into Christianity. With the establishment of colonial rule, five villages of the Zeliangrong Nagas were located within the British Reserve Area of Imphal town; they are the present Keishamthong, Moirangkhom, Kakhulong, Majorkhul and Ragailong. The tribal employees of the Manipur State Police including band party were settled in Keishamthong. The employees of the Political Agency, Medical department and Gurkha Rifles were settled in the localities of Kakhulong, Majorkhul and Ragailong. The people of these Zeliangrong villages performed their festivals particularly Gaan Ngai festival with great enthusiasm. The Zeliangrong elders still narrate that the British officers did not look towards them with sympathy over the performance of Gaan Ngai festival particularly beating of the drums at night which disturbed their sleep. Meiphunlung Golmei, an elder of Majorkhul told the father of the author that one Charles Jaffery, the state engineer felt greatly annoyed at the beating of the drums by the youths of Majorkhul. He rushed to the village and confisticated the drums and other musical instruments and prohibited dancing and singing or ho-hoing during the Gaan Ngai festival. Of course it was compromised later on. The Maharaja of Manipur and his noble men did not disturb the performance of the Gaan Ngai dances. The Hindu Meitei as a whole welcomed the Gaa Ngai festival. Some adventurous among them visited the Naga villages to see the dances and participated in the festivities. Some Meitei elders described even now the Gaan Ngai as Wakching kummei/ haraoba (festival of the month of Wakching). But majority of the Meiteis described Gaan Ngai as Hao Haraoba (festival of the tribals).

During the colonial period, many Zelaingrong Nagas entered into the lower grades of services and they faced extreme difficulties in participating in the Gaan Ngai festival during the office hours. Therefore the youth and girls dormitory had to make programme to suit the presence of the employee elders. There was a felt necessity that the Zeliangrong government servants might get relaxation in their office time during Gaan Ngai festival. During the last days of the Second World War in 1945 there were many European soldiers mostly English and American who observed the Gaan Ngai festival and participated in eating and drinking in the villages. At the end of the Second World War the Zeliangrong people throughout their respective villages in Assam, Manipur and Naga Hills observed this post harvest festival. Some of the Zeme elders saw the performance of the Gaan Ngai, dancing and singing in Kohima and similarity between Rongmei and Zeme was noticed. Most of the villages in western hills of Manipur ranging from Tamenglong Khunjao village to Khoupum valley performed the Gaan Ngai festival. The Christian missionaries who were mostly indigenous persons banned the festival, performance of dances and singing of songs and putting on of traditional clothes and costumes. This orthodox prohibition of the Baptist missionary did a lot of damage to the tribal culture. At the time of India's independence the community leaders established two organizations namely, Kabui Naga Association and Zeliangrong Council. They converted the Kabui Naga Association into the Manipur Zeliangrong Union in December 1947. The Kabui Naga Association prepared a set of customs known as Kabui customs. This handbook on Kabui custom was enforced by the Manipur Zelaingrong Union throughout the post colonial period. The Kabui Naga Association passed a resolution fixing the performance of the Gaan Ngai festival on 13th day of Manipuri month of Wakching which coincides with the month of Pous of Sakabda Era. It took more than half a century for the people to accept this date. The followers of the traditional religion had to observe many gennas or neihmeis at the local level. Therefore the emergence of common date for the performance of Gaan Ngai was greatly delayed.

After independence the performance of the Gaan Ngai festival had become more liberal. Gennas were relaxed; many outsiders particularly the Naga tribesmen and Meitei spectators were freely allowed to observe the Gaan Ngai festival. A healthy practice of inviting guests to attend the Gaan Ngai feast at the community or individual houses had become very popular. The guests included the Hindus, the Christians, the Meiteis, the Indian communities, other Naga tribes and Kukis. The Zeliangrong community was more exposed to the outsiders during this festival. The Zeliangrong dance forms, popularly known as Kabui Naga dance was learnt by Meitei dancers. The state government encouraged the performance of the indigenous dances during state festivals mostly folk dance festivals of Republic of India. The practice of performance of Zeliangrong dances in the villages whenever an official dignitary visited was revived. The Christian missionaries who were orthodox followers of Baptist Christianity had become more liberal. The revival of the indigenous or traditional form of art was encouraged by the state government. The Zeliangrong festivals had become all communities affair and gradually it took a secular form.

Secularization of the Gaan Ngai festival made a land mark when some Zeliangrong political activists of the Indian National Congress approached Chief Minister Rajkumar Dorendra Singh to give a holiday for the Gaan Ngai festival. The Government of Manipur declard the Gaan Ngai festival as a Restricted Holiday since 1976. There was popular demand that Gaan Ngai should be given official recognition by making it as a General Holiday for the state of Manipur. There was difference of opinion between the Christian Naga leaders and the Zeliangrong indigenous religion group on this issue. The Christian leaders thought that as the Government of Manipur had given a General Holiday for the artificially created Naga festival known as "Lui Ngai Ni", there was no need for another holiday for a particular Naga community. There is also a holiday for the Kuki-Chin festival of Kut. The Zeliangrong Religious Council which was founded in 1994 pleaded for declaration of Gaan Ngai festival as a holiday. So in 1998 during the Chief Ministership of W. Nipamacha Singh in whose cabinet Prof. Gangmumei Kamei a Zeliangrong leader was associated declared Gaan Ngai as a State Holiday. The Government of Manipur declared on 27th December 1997, "In partial modification of this government order of even no. dated 27-11-97, the Government of Manipur is pleased to declare 10th January 1998 which falls on 2nd Saturday on account of the Gaan Ngai festival". The Zelaingrong Religious Council organized a big Gaan Ngai festival in which the ministers of Manipur led by Chief Minister W. Nipamacha Singh participated irrespective of their creed and caste. The Zeliangrong community presented their traditional clothes, Phei Ngao as gifts to all the ministers of the Government. The Chief Minister of Manipur also distributed red blankets to the elders present. The observation was held at the Rongmei village of Ragailong on 10th January 1998. The decision of Nipamacha Singh's Government declaring a General Holiday was welcomed by the people generally. On 7th November 1998, the Government declared the Gaan Ngai as a holiday for all banks and financial institutions in Manipur under the Negotiable Act, 1881 over and above all offices and educational institutions on account of Gaan Ngai festival.

It was later on found out that a section of Christian Indian National Congress leaders led by some interested persons were opposed to this step. It came out in 2002 when O. Ibobi Singh was made the Chief Minister and those Christian Congress leaders became members of the council of ministers. The Government of Manipur cancelled the Gaan Ngai holiday and it led to a great controversy.

Controversy over the Deletion of General Holiday of Gaan Ngai

The controversy was created by the Government of Manipur headed by O. Ibobi Singh. Chaoba Kamson who was the most vociferous leader against this government move made the following observations.

Then, the SPF Govt. headed by Shri O. Ibobi Singh came into power and unfortunately struck off the Gaan Ngai from the State Holiday List, 2003 by a cabinet meeting dated 20-10-2002. The Zeliangrong people already enjoyed holiday for the last 5 years in the name of Gaan Ngai Festival. The unpopular cabinet decision shocked and hurt the sentiment of Zeliangrong people. There was a hue and cry against the decision of the Ibobi Government.

It might not be his intention to delete this festival– from the Holiday list of 2003 but he was influenced by his coterie. The eight organizations belonging to Zeliangrong community had formed a committee called, "Demand Committee on Restoration of Gaan Ngai Holiday" with Shri Meibon Phaomei as the convenor. Zeliangrong United Club Association Manipur Valley (ZUCAMV) and Zeliangrong Religious Council had submitted a memorandum dated 31-10-2002 and 05-11-2002 respectively separately to the Hon'ble Chief Minister of Manipur to review immediately the cabinet decision and reinstate the Gaan Ngai Festival in the State Holiday List, 2003. Again on 09-11-2002, a joint memorandum signed by the leaders of (1) Zeliangrong Religious Council, Assam, Manipur and Nagaland, (2) Zeliangrong Union, Assam, Manipur and Nagaland, (3) Zeliangrong Students' Union, Manipur, (4) All Zeliangrong Arts and Cultural Organization [AZACO], (5) Zeliangrong Women's Society, Manipur Valley, (6) Zeliangrong Youth Front, (7) Zeliangrong United Club Association Manipur Valley [ZUCAMV] and (8) Zeliangrong Cultural Council was submitted to the Hon'ble Chief Minister of Manipur requesting to review the unjustified cabinet decision and restore the Gaan Ngai Festival in the General Holiday List, 2003 for unity and integrity of Manipur.

Prominent personalities namely His Highness, the Maharaja of Manipur Sanajaoba Leisemba, Shri Sameul Jendai, hon'ble MLA and Councilors of Imphal Municipal Council had appealed the Government of Manipur to roll back the cabinet decision for all the interest of the society. A number of social organizations like (1) UCM, (2) AMUCO, (3) AMSU, (4) MSF, (5) Kuki Inpi Manipur [KIM], (6) League of the Fourth World People [NE Region], (7) United Naga Council [UNC], (8) Ethno Heritage Council, (9) Lainingthou Sanamahi Thougal Kanglup, (10) Meira Paibi Lup, (11)

Kangleipak Langjing Apunba Meira Lup, (12) All Manipur Ethnical Socio-Cultural Organization, (13) Tarahei Youth Development Organization, (14) Manipur Peace and Integrity Council [MAPI], (15) Koren [Koireng] Youth Organization, (16) ANSAM, (17) AMKL, (18) ISTV, (19) AIR, Imphal Station, and (20) All Manipur Action Committee, Wangoi, issued statements in favour of restoration of Gaan Ngai Festival in the Holiday list, 2003. Local newspapers played a leading role to restore this festival in the Holiday list, 2003 by writing in editorial columns highlighting the necessity to retain the same for the best interest of Manipur.

The controversy over Gaan Ngai was boon in disguise. While exposing the political elements opposed to the Zeliangrong community it draws a great support from all sections of the society irrespective of ethnic groups, religious denominations and political parties. This controversy made the Gaan Ngai as all community affair. The Governemnt led by O. Ibobi Singh changed its mind and restored the holiday. This controversy has made the Gaan Ngai a secular affair going beyond the religious boundaries of the Zeliangrong community. The statements of different groups and personalities, editorials and memoranda on this controversy issue reflect how every section of Manipur society and public opinion is in support of Gaan Ngai festival. Gaan Ngai Celebration Committee, Manipur published a collection of articles on Gaan Ngai, press cuttings and documents which can be regarded as a documentation of the Gaan Ngai controversy in history. Some selected documents are reproduced below.

The Zeliangrong United Club Association Manipur Valley (ZUCAMV) submitted a seven point representation to Shri O. Ibobi Singh, Chief Minister of Manipur dated 31-10-2002 became the core issue statements of controversy. The representation declared that "Gaan Ngai is the biggest

Zeliangrong festival celebrated by Zeme, Liangmai, Rongmei and Puimei with slight differences of nomenclature. The passing generation from the olden days of ancestors has also contributed certain developments in the evolution of pronounciations and dialectic accents i.e.

1. Zemes celebrate Gaan Ngai as Hega Ngi
2. Liangmais celebrate Gaan Ngai as Gin Ngai (Chaga Ngi)
3. Rongmeis celebrate as Gaan Ngai
4. Puimeis celebrate as Gaan Ngai

The ZUCAMV asked the Chief Minister to restore Gaan Ngai festival as a General Holiday from 16th January 2003.

Immediately the Maharaja of Manipur Sanajaoba Leisemba supported the demand for the restoration of Gaan Ngai holiday. It was reported on 1-11-2002 in Sangai Express.

"Public outcry against the recent State Cabinet decision of deleting Gaan Ngai festival from the list of General Holiday is becoming more intense with many organizations and individual voicing their unhappiness and reservations over the decision.

"His Highness the Maharaja of Manipur Sanajaoba Leisemba joining the tirade against the Govt.'s decision of deleting Gaan Ngai from the general holiday list has termed it as very unfortunate and a challenge to the integrity of the state.

"What could be construed from such a move apart from destabilizing the state, if the present Govt. failed to recognize the importance of the festival of the Kabui tribe who have been living in peaceful coexistence with other group of people since time immemorial, the Maharaja said in a press release and demanded revocation of the Cabinet decision in the general interest of the public".

Two organizations, civil societies of Manipur, All Manipur United Clubs Organization (AMUCO) and United Committee Manipur (UCM) which had been visiting the Zeliangrong villages in Manipur valley to exchange gifts of clothes, fruits and sweet meats on the occasion of Gaan Ngai strongly supported the demand of the Zeliangrong people and were involved in mobilizing the public opinion in favour of Gaan Ngai festival. The press in Manipur both in English and Manipuri criticized the decision of the Government and demanded for the restoration of holiday. The Imphal Free Press wrote an editorial in favour of Gaan Ngai dated 4-11-2002 in the caption of Paid Holidays. "There is no gainsaying that the Manipur Govt. has too many scheduled as well as unscheduled holidays. But while this is true, we are at a loss why it decided to cancel the traditional holiday on one of the major festivals of a major community in the state Gaan Ngai of the Kabuis. By the Manipur Govt.'s holiday logic which lays a premium on festivals, there cannot be a case for a holiday more genuine than the Gaan Ngai. Ideally we would have preferred the Govt. holiday list to be rationalized on the basis of the universality of the festival under consideration with those not falling under this category accorded just a restricted holiday status. If this norm were to be applied, a lot many of the days the state observes as holiday, would become just restricted holidays, saving itself numerous man hours. Considering the state Govt. spends about Rs. 2.5 crores daily on salaries of its employees alone, this is not a matter of joke. We would estimate that the Govt. employees on the average are paid 12 months salaries for ten or less months of haft hearted work after taking into account the scheduled holidays as well as the bandh and cease ork strikes which have become a staple of the state. If the Govt. had been a private enterprise, keenly aware of its daily balance sheet, this consciousness would have dawned much more quickly and effectively. But then the attitude today is govt. employment is itself a euphemism for paid holiday. The govt. should try and find out how much daily wage earners and small marginal businesses abhor holidays and bandh to get a rough idea of what the story on the other side of its cocooned wolrd is. Jokes apart, we are even of the opinion that religious holidays should be avoided as far as possible, so that state holidays are more in the nature of neutral rest days for workers. But the tradition has been as in the case of so many other agenda in the state to treat even holidays on considerations of political correctness and appeasement. Hence the effort or call it pressure, has been to distribute state holidays proportionately amongst the different communities living in the state. We underscore the point again. As long as this is the norm, Gaan Ngai is no less an occasion for a holiday than any other holiday". This is a sensible editorial which gave guarded support to Gaan Ngai.

After two months of protess, processions, public meetings, statements and counter statements, the Government of Manipur restored the Gaan Ngai in a cabinet meeting held on 12th November 2002. The convenor of the Demand Committee on restoration of Gaan Ngai holiday, Meibon Phaomei issued a press release of gratitude to all the voluntary organizations, electronic and print media, volunteers of both hill and valley and particularly Maharaja Sanajaoba Leisemba for all out support extended towards the restoration of Gaan Ngai holiday. The Zeliangrong Rachapriak Phom (Zeliangrong Religious Council, Assam, Manipur and Nagaland) notified that the Government had restored the holiday and it requested all the village councils to celebrate this festival simultaneously on 16th January 2003. Thus the battle of restoration of Gaan Ngai was won. The Zeliangrong Religious Council restated "Gaan Ngai is a greatest living festival of the Zeliangrong people...It is a traditional, cultural and religious festival celebrating from time immemorial. In this festival, rites and rituals are performed to Tingkao Ragwang to shower His blessings for peace and prosperity on earth and pay due homage to the departed souls so that the souls may rest in heavenly abode".

Gaan Ngai celebration as a State Function

The great landmark in the modernization of Gaan Ngai was held with the observation of Gaan Ngai festival on 16th January 2003. The public opinion was that there was no proper understanding of Gaan Ngai festival by non Zeliangrong community. It was proposed to showcase the festival by performing it as a state level function. A Gaan Ngai Celebration Committee Manipur was constituted to organize the festival. The following were the members of the committee.

1.	G. Moirangjao, Ex-Chairperson of Imphal Municipal Council	Chairman
2.	M. Maringa, Ex-Municipal Councillor of Imphal	Vice-Chairman
3.	Chaoba Kamson General Secretary of Zeliangrong Religious Council Assam, Manipur and Nagaland	Secretary
4.	Poudongai Kamson	Joint Secretary
5.	Meibon Phaomei, President ZUCAMV	Joint Secretary
6.	Poubilung Dangmei	Joint Secretary
7.	Abungba Longmei	Joint Secretary
8.	Kanetlu Dangmei	Joint Secretary

Funds were collected as donations from the public to meet the expenses of the festival. The proposed state level festival raised an important issue. Traditionally, the Gaan Ngai was performed in the villages and they were organized by the boys' amd girls' dormitories under the supervision of village council. The individual households also participated in the festival. The state level function was to be organized by a community level committee without any religious or social status. For the state level Gaan Ngai festival of 2003, it was performed at the Bhagyachandra Open Air Theatre run by the Government. The celebration committee took the responsibility of organizing it. The participants were the Zeliangrong people who were invited from the Zeliangrong villages in the Manipur valley. Invitations were issued by the celebration committee to guests consisting of officials and non officials without consideration of creed and status. The Gaan Ngai festival in the villages was performed without special guests. In this state level function, His Excellency Shri Ved Marwah, Governor of Manipur was invited to be the Chief Guest; O. Ibobi Singh, the Chief Minister of Manipur who restord the Gaan Ngai holiday was the President of the function and W. Nipamacha Singh, a former Chief Minister during whose tenure Gaan Ngai was declared a state holiday was the Guest of Honour. Several former ministers, MLAs and high officials attended the function.

It was a one day state function. It was a secular occasion consisting of state level guests. It was a trend setter for celebrating the state level Gaan Ngai. The function started with a group hymn sung by women members of the Zeliangrong Religious Council by singing "Tingkao Ragwang hai gaiye". It was followed by the group ho-hoing shouted by the youth of the villages of Imphal. The traditional head dress (Chei), ceremonial costumes and spears were presented by the Chairman of the celebration committee to His Excellency Shri Ved Marwah Governor of Manipur, Chief Minister O. Ibobi Singh and former Chief Minister W. Nipamacha Singh. A new fire was produced by the method of wood and bamboo pieces friction by the volunteer youth. Gaan Ngai was regarded as the end of the year but this new fire gave the message of the coming New Year. The welcome and dances were performed at the beautifully decorated stage of the Bhagyachandra Open Air Theatre. Khullakpa Athoumu Kamson of Kakhulong presented beating of the drum followed by singing of "Ra luh".

The dignitaries who graced the occasion rose to the occasion to express the spirit and message of Gaan Ngai festival. His Excellency Shri Ved Marwah Governor of Manipur addressed the crowd at the Open Air Theatre. He said he was overwhelmed by the beauty and spiritual message of the opening hymns sung by the women folk. He expressed his happiness at being invited to such a big Naga festival. He gave a message of good will to the people of Manipur to live in peace and prosperity on this occasion. Chief Minister O. Ibobi Singh expressed his happiness to get this opportunity to attend the Gaan Ngai festival which was held for the first time as a state level function. He informed that the Gaan Ngai festival would be a state holiday in Manipur as a respect to the Zeliangrong people and their great festival of Gaan Ngai. He extended monetary gifts for the organizers of the festival. Former Chief Minister W. Nipamacha Singh was cheered by the crowd when he went up the stage to address the well attired Zeliangrong audience. He told the gathering that Gaan Ngai is a living cultural festival of an indigenous people. Therefore, it was proper to acknowledge this living festival by declaring it a state holiday. He was happy that Chief Minister O. Ibobi Singh has restored the state holiday. He described the decision of Ibobi Singh as a wise and statesman like decision. Manipur state should respect each and every community living in the state irrespective of its population, religion and culture. After the opening ceremony, several dancing and singing groups performed their dances. It was a memorable day for the Zeliangrong people and the leaders of the state of Manipur. Boys and girls putting on their best attire performed their beautiful dances of the Gaan

Ngai festival. Musical instruments like drum, gong, cymbal and 'Ra' were played with skill by the experienced artist. Some modern fashion minded people organized a beautiful fashion show presenting both male and female dresses with beautiful model like youths. This function was historic in the sense that Gaan Ngai was organized at the state level including of course the festival in the villages.

Subsequently the state level Gaan Ngai festival was organized at different places and villages throughout the valley of Imphal. The Gaan Ngai celebration committee had done a great service to the popularity of this festival. The committee published several books and handouts related to the Gaan Ngai festival. After the winding up of the celebration committee, the responsibility of the Gaan Ngai festival was taken over by a cultural organization named, All Zeliangrong Arts and Culture Organization (AZACO). They organized the festival at different places including far of villages. For example, in 2012 the AZACO organized the Gaan Ngai festival at the foothill village of Chiningkhol of Sadar Hills sub division. The Chief Guest of the function was the President of United Committee of Manipur. This year another secular organization known as The Zeliangrong Union organized the state level Gaan Ngai festival at the Bhagyachandra Open Air Theatre at Imphal. The celebration did not include the ritualistic aspect which was performed at a nearby village. His Excellency Gurbachan Jagat, the Governor of Manipur was the Chief Guest and Shri L.P. Gonmei, IAS, Additional Chief Secretary of Manipur was the President of the function. This is a clear case of secularization of the Gaan Ngai festival and it is welcomed by every section of the society.

In the performance of Hega Ngi festival of Zeliangrong Heraka, this festival was attended by officials, guests, social workers of other faiths. In Assam Hega Ngi had already become all community affair both official and non official. In Cachar valley during the Gaan Ngai festival many non

Naga people joined the festival in the villages. Among the Liangmai section of the Zeliangrong group who had left their indigenous religion performed the Chaga Ngi now popularly known as Chaga Gadi was organized by the people without religious rituals. The Governemnt of Nagaland declared the Chaga Gadi on 31st October as a state holiday. Many Christian converts attended the Chaga Gadi. There was also a strong move started by Christian intellectuals to observe the Chaga Gadi as the moral and spiritual values of Chaga Gadi are needed by modern people. They even identified the similarity of the Christian values with Zeliangrong values in terms of sharing each other pleasure, charity and endevour for prosperity.

In Nagaland several Rongmeis who were converts into Christianity desire to revive Gaan Ngai festival without the religious performances. In Jalukie valley, the Christian Rongmeis performed the Gaan Ngai festival by dancing and singing secular dances and songs. People desire to revive the Gaan Ngai. This naturally would strengthen the modernizing process of Gaan Ngai. Gaan Ngai is looked upon now as a cultural expression of the Zeliangrong people. After going through the process of social change in Zeliangrong society it is felt that festivals, dances, ceremonies need to be preserved for the sustenance of the Zeliangrong culture.

Chief Minister W. Nipamacha Singh of Manipur with Minister Prof. Gangmumei Kamei and Thaninjao Remei performing Laogai Karikmei ceremony of Gaan Ngai Festival on 10th January, 1998 at Ragailong, Imphal

Ministers of Manipur at the Gaan Ngai Feast at Ragailong, Imphal

His Excellency Shri Ved Marwah, Governor of Manipur as Chief Guest of Gaan Ngai Festival on 16th January, 2003 at Imphal

Chief Minister O. Ibobi Singh of Manipur speaking at the Gaan Ngai Festival on 16th January 2003

VIPs at Gaan Ngai Festival on 16th January 2003 at Imphal

His Excellency Shri Gurbachan Jagat Governor of Manipur at the Gaan Ngai 2012

Spectators of Gaan Ngai 2012 at Chinikon Village

Gaan Ngai 2012 at Chinikon Village

ANNEXURE 1

The profiles of the Zeliangrong community, religion and festivals including the Gaan Ngai based on the questionares responded to by the research consultants.

Chaoba Kamson responded to the questionaire given below:

1.	Name of the Respondent	-	Chaoba Kamson
(a)	Qualification	-	Graduate (Arts)
(b)	Occupation & Profession	-	Govt. employee
(c)	Social and Religious activities	-	General Secretary, Tingkao Ragwang Chapriak Phom, Assam, Manipur and Nagaland
2.	Name of the community	-	Rongmei of Zeliangrong group

(a) What are the cognate groups of the Zelaingrong?

They are Zeme, Liangmai, Rongmei and Puimei

(b) Is the respondent aware of the Zeliangrong Solidarity Movement?

Yes

(c) If yes, give a brief account

For solidarity of Zeliangrong, the leaders of Zeme, Liangmai and Rongmei coined a new nomenclature as Zeliangrong on 15th February 1947 at Keishamthong Imphal (composite name of Zeme, Liangmai and Rongmei). The new organization was called as the "Zeliangrong Council". Again on 30th November 1980, Zeliangrong Peoples' Convention (ZPC) was formed to amalgamate the Zeliangrong inhabited areas of Assam, Manipur and Nagaland under a common political roof. ZPC submitted a series of memorandum to the then president of India, the then Prime Minister of India and other Ministers of India demanding to unite all the contiguous Zeliangrong inhabited areas of Assam, Manipur and Nagaland into a common political administration. Besides, a number of agitations such as bandh, blockade, rally, public meeting etc. were launched under the able leadership of prof. Gangmumei Kamei. So, this agitation is known as Zeliangrong Solidarity Movement.

3. What are the religious beliefs of the Zeliangrong community?

The religious beliefs among the Zeliangrong community are (1) Tingkao Ragwang Chapriak (TRC), (2) Heraka Religion and (3) Christianity.

4. Give an account of the Zeliangrong Heraka Religion.

Heraka literaly means in Zeme pure or 'not inpure'. 'Hera' means smaller deities, 'Ka' means fence or give up. So small gods must be avoided and only the supreme God, Tingwang must be worshipped. The followers of Heraka believe the concept of monotheism, that is, worship of Tingwang only. The main concept of Heraka religion will be blessed good fortune in their life. The immortal souls of good doers will go to God's kingdom. They believe the concept of rebirth.

Mode of worship

The way of worship in Heraka religion is simple. It is a devotional worshipping. Prayer may be performed individually or collectively at any time and day. Any individual may offer prayer at morning, day, evening before sleep. They peactice and pray at Kelumki. The system of Heraka prayer at Kelumki on the full moon-day and the Heraka New Year Day are as follows:

1. Gathering at Kelumki early in the morning
2. Recitation of Mantra and offering of Mass Prayer led by a priest
3. Singing devotional songs inside Kelumki
4. Individual prayer at the holy alter
5. Singing of benedictory song
6. Singing a rejoicing song in praise of the Supreme God
7. Exultant prayer by the priest upon the offertories
8. Singing a devotional song followed by incantation of Heraka Mantra
9. Taking of Telau dui (holy water) on the Heraka New Year Day

Who was the founder of Heraka and who are the followers of this cult?

Rani Gaidinliu was the founder of Heraka Religion. Zeliangrong people are the main followers of this religion.

5. What is the Tingkao Ragwang Chapriak (TRC) of the Zeliangrong? Give a brief account of this religious system.

Tingkao Ragwang Chapriak (TRC) is a name of Zeliangrong religion which was christened on 16-04-1994 at Imphal by the Zeliangrong people of Assam, Manipur and Nagaland. The followers of TRC believe the concept of polytheism, the concept of Supreme God, the concept of life after death, the concept of thundijang, the concept of Taroiram, the concept of Heaven, the concept of sin, bliss and rebirth, ancestor worship etc. In TRC faith there are two types of worship of Tingkao Ragwang. First the followers of TRC pray to Tingkao Ragwang with offerings. Another type is prayer to Him without any offerings. Prayers without offerings are Munthimmei, Lumthengmei, Mhailu Bammei and Ganthengkai kumei. These prayers are fasting invoking the Supreme God for well being of mankind.

6. Please mention the names of the festivals performed by the cognate groups of the Zeliangrong people. Month or season of the performance of the festivals.

	Name of festival of Rongmei	*Month*	*Season*
1.	Gaan-Ngai	Dec-Jan	Winter
2.	Rih-Ngai	Jan-Feb	Winter
3.	Nanu-Ngai	Feb-March	Spring
4.	Longnapkaodai	Feb-March	Spring
5.	Gin-ki-Ngai	April	Spring
6.	Gudui-Ngai (Maleng-Ngai)	May	Summer
7.	Tun-Ngai	July-August	Summer
8.	Pukpha-Ngai	Aug-Sept.	Autumn
9.	Dongjao-Ngai	December	Winter
10.	Ten-Ngai	December	Winter

(b) Significance of the festivals

Zeliangrong people celebrate all kinds of festivals when the moon ascends but never observe them when the moon descends. Gaan-Ngai festival is celebrated mainly by the believers of TRC and Heraka religion. They celebrate this festival for the living and the dead. Religious, cultural and customary activities signifying the identity of Zeliangrong are prominently performed. Rih-Ngai is the war victory festival. Nanu-Ngai is for the fertility to produce more offsprings. Longnapkaodai means calling of paddy and also known as seed sowing festival celebrated for one day. Ginki Ngai is the worship and entertainment of goddess of wealth (paddy) for plentiful food grain. Gudui-Ngai means ginger soup drinking festival and it is also worship of Tingkao Ragwang for plentiful harvest. Every household sacrifices a cock and its intestine is hung at the wall of the house. Tun-Ngai literally means festival of rainy season. During this festival, villagers carry out social services like clearance of village pod, path leading to the paddy field and cut the bushes which outgrow the path. Festive spirit is poor in this festival comparing to other festivals. Pukpha-Ngai is a festival of new crop tasting which celebrates in the month of July-August every year. It is believed that on this particular day of festival everyone should take their meal to full satisfaction otherwise, one will feel hungry throughout the year. Dongjao-Ngai (Banchat Ngai) means watching of the granary festival. The villagers led by elderly man will visit every household shouting rilai hoi and see every granary who has produced the highest quantity of paddy. Every house owner will produce chutney of vegetables or meat with holy wine. After offering of holy wine to Tingkao Ragwang, all the villagers will eat the chutney and drink the wine. Ten-Ngai means bread tasting festival which usually celebrates in the month of December. Boys and girls will grind the wet rice for making bread. They make the bread at girls' dormitory. After finishing, all the members of boys' and girls' dormitories will eat the bread and koutenji at boys' dormitory.

(c) Give a brief description of each of the festivals

(i) Gaan Ngai – It is the living and greatest festival of Zeliangrong people of north east India. It is a religious, cultural and identity festival celebrated by the devotees of TRC and Heraka Religion. It is a festival of the living and the dead lasting for at least 5 days. Rites and rituals are performed such as offering of ginger and eggs to the presiding deities, calling of paddy to restore the consumed or wasted rice, ritual act at the northern gate on the last day of the festival performed to all gods believed and worshipped by the Zeliangrong people.

Oblation of holy wine to Tingkao Ragwang before lunch and supper is offered. After dance, holy wine is also offered to the Supreme God. Cultural activities like dancing, singing, drum beating, shouting of hoi etc. are performed. Customary works like admission of new members to boys' and girls' dormitories, admission of newly wedded wife to married women's dormitory, promotion from Khangbon to Gaanchang, Gaanchang to Banja, Banja to Khunbu or Khunlak, from married women to old women are done. Any vacant post lying is filled up on the last day of the festival. Sports activities are performed on the first day of the festival.

(ii) Rih-Ngai – It means war (victory) festival. Generally, it is celebrated for one day but some villages celebrate this festival for 2 to 3 days. Ritual called Lumthengmei for purification of one's body, mind and soul is performed for making oneself good fortune for every challenges of life for war, hunting etc. In some villages, males do not eat foods prepared by women so they themselves prepare foods and cook at the village gate on the 2nd or 3rd day of the festival. There is no feasting at the dormitory in this festival. Ritaak Ganmei is performed at the northern and southern gates of the village by two or three elderly men holding a spear each reciting war hymns.

(iii) Nanu-Ngai – It is an important festival of ear piercing of the children born in the preceding year. The ears of the children are pierced. It is also a fertility festival for the birth of more offsprings and to have a fruitful cultivation in the village. In the early morning of the day, the old women fetch water from the village pond for washing the baby and cooking for ritual purposes. The ceremony of Najum Gaimei will be performed by the village old men with a cock and a hen called Sangdai and Sanglou to Tingkao Ragwang for blessing the child with a bright future, long life, prosperity, success, victory over the enemies etc. The cock and the hen are cooked for Nashan Kanmei ritual. After the ritual, ears of the children will be pierced with a needle called Nanu Roumei. The members of the boys' dormitory distribute mud to every household of the village for bountiful food grain for the coming year. After that the boys holding a long bamboo and starting from the traditional institution called Nek Kaibang will march singing a ritual song 'Tulamroi, Tulamroi'. The march will halt for a while at southern gate and proceed to northern gate. Then the fertility song for more production of children will be sung by the boys' dormitory. The old men and women who perform dance singing the traditional songs also sing the same song at the house of the children. On the next day of the festival, a complete genna called Nashang Nei is observed to avert death at delivery in the village.

(iv) Longnapkaodai – This festival is the calling of the paddy. It is also known as seed sowing festival celebrated for one day in the month of February-March. It is the festival of worship of Tingkao Ragwang for plentiful harvest. A big pig along with a cock is sacrificed in the name of Tingkao Ragwang for rich crop of the year. This ritual is performed at the residence of Napmupou who is incharge of agricultural rite of the village. Nobody will sow the seeds in the field till the Napmupou does. The spleen of the pig will be observed carefully to find out whether any bad or good omen reflects thereon. The victim is roasted and cut into many pieces for distribution to every household. Any individual house may also performe the ritual of calling of paddy by sacrificing a cock towards evening on that day. A small piece of land of Napmupou will be dg out to sow the seeds with related hymns. If the seeds sprout out well, it is certain that a rich harvest in the year will be availed of otherwise a poor harvest. After this, individual house can sow the seeds at their respective paddy field. The cooked liver of the cock will be placed on the three stones of the hearth for a good harvest. The three stones of the hearth represent the goddess (a) Kambuipui, (b) Charaipui and (c) Kairao (ancestors).

(v) Ginki-Ngai – It is the worship and festing of the goddess of paddy or wealth for more procurement of food grain. The word, Gin means guest, Ki means entertainment of the guest. The name of the goddess is called Kangdailu (Mailailu). It is a one day festival held in the month of March-April. The ritual of Napchanmei is usually performed only by women. According to legendary, "One day Kangdailu, goddess of food in charge disguised herself in the form of an old woman wearing worn out clothes visited every house requesting to hold one night. The house owner refused her request on the plea that they had a new calf so they were under a religious genna. At last she approached to a house where two orphans lived. The two orphans said that they had no objection to her stay one night there but they had nothing to feed the visiting old woman who was supposed to be hungry. Inspite of this, she told them to look inside the bin of grain (napshaam pantilai) whether single rice was available or not. Accordingly they took out a single rice and cooked the same. Thereafter, Kangdailu ordered them to prepare curry. They said that they had nothing to cook for curry also. She took out a crab and put it in the curry pot. The curry pot was full of crabs. Thus, they had dined together that evening. A mat of bamboo was arranged for her sleep. On the mat, a huge quantity of paddy was piled up for the orphans. Just before her departure in the morning, she advised the orphans to sow some seeds in the paddy field and remaining portion of paddy would be used for ritual purpose i.e. calling of paddy. Saying this, she left the village. They persuaded her to live together with them but she refused saying that divine and mankind could not always live together. The villagers also came to know that the old woman was no other than but Kangdailu. In the Ginki Ngai, crab is compulsory among the food items. Out of this story, Zeliangrong people observe Ginki Ngai every year for plentiful food grain.

(vi) Gudui Ngai – Gudui Ngai meaning the ginger soup drinking festival is celebrated in the month of April-May for one day only. Early in the morning of the festival every household performs a ritual called Maleng Keimei with an offering of rice beer and crushed ginger to Tingkao Ragwang followed by a ritual of calling of paddy. After the performance of this ritual, the legs of the cock are observed in search of good sign. The intestine of the victim is removed and hung at the wall of the house. It is hung to be seen by the mother goddess called Kangdailu. If she sees the hanging of intestine, she is pleased to distribute the paddy grain for the coming year. Tug of war for bountiful harvest is carried out between boys and girls at the courtyard of the male dormitory. Katu Luh is sung to drive away the pests and insects from the paddy field. The objective of this festival is to grow the paddy plants properly and nourish and roots to the soil, expand its stem quickly not causing any harm by insects and pests etc. On the following day, a genna called 'Dikap Nei' is observed by abstaining from earth or muddy works.

(vii) Tun Ngai – It is celebrated in the rainy season. Its main objective is to clean the village pond, the path leading to paddy field and cut the bushes which outgrow the path etc. with a prayer to Tingkao Ragwang for prosperity. Like Gaan Ngai festival, rituals, dancing, singing, traditional drum beating and other cultural activities are performed in this festival.

(viii) Pukpha Ngai – It is a new crop tasting festival celebrated for one day only either in the month of July-August. The new crop is offered to Tingkao Ragwang before man consumes. Nowadays, Napkaomei ceremony is performed at individual's family by a priest for good harvest. It is believed that on this particular day of festival everyone should eat with full satisfaction otherwise one will feel hungry throughout the year.

(ix) Dongjao Ngai – In this festival, the villagers go and watch the granary of every house shouting hoi. One who produces the highest quantity of paddy is called Muleng Lamei and 2nd position is known as Mulengna Lamei. When shouting of hoi ends, holy wine is offered to Tingkao Ragwang for well being and prosperity of the family. Then the participants eat the chutney of vegetables and drink wine prepared by the house owner. The act of watching of granary is not carried out to those who have no granaries.

(x) Ten Ngai – Ten Ngai means bread tasting festival which celebrates in the early part of December after new crops are stored in granary. Nowadays, celebration of this festival is in minimum except some villages. Every member of girls' dormitory will bring some quantity of rice as their share for preparartion of bread and koutenji. Koutenji means boiled bread made of rice flour packed with banana leaf. The bread and koutnji will be prepared at girls' dormitory. After preparation the girls will bring those breads and koutenji at the boys' dormitory. The head of boys' and girls' dormitory and all members present will eat the same. Boys also catch fishes and hunt wild animals. They cooked and eat them together in the evening. After food, boys and girls sing folk songs at boys' dormitory till day breaks. It is an interesting festival but celebration id held poorly. Some Zeliangrong villages are still celebrating this festival. So this festival is an essential part of religion. Regular observation of festivals can survive and sustain the rich traditional religion, custom and culture.

7. In what villages of the cognate groups of the Zeliangrong community the Gaan Ngai festival is performed? What are the equivalent names of this festival among the Zeme, Liangmai and Rongmei?

Gaan Ngai is mainly celebrated in the Zeliangrong villages by the followers of indigenous religion of Tingkao Ragwang Chapriak and Heraka Religion. The equivalent names of this festival among Zeme, Liangmai and Rongmei are as follows.

Gaan Ngai is called Gaan Ngai among the Rongmei (Kabui), Hegangi among the Zeme and Gin Ngai among the Liangmai.

8. Give a brief description of the different days of the festival among the Zeme, Liangmai and Rongmei.

The different days of the Gaan Ngai festival among the Rongmeis are given at the answer number nine. Regarding the different days of the festival among Zeme and Liangmai, I have no idea.

9. Give a description of the respective days of the festival in your village.

(i) The First Day – Ngaigangmei

The first day of the festival is called Ngaigangmei which means beginning of the festival. Early in the morning, a ritual of Gucheng Phaimei is performed invoking the village presiding deities to give well being and not to happen any kind of disturbances during the festival. It is followed by offering of holy wine to Tingkao Ragwang at boys' dormitory. Then boys will beat drum which means heralding of the festival. A pig is scarificed in the name of Tingkao Ragwang and its spleen will be examined to know the omen of the future. The victim is cooked and a curry of Zeigan made of internal parts of the victim with its blood is separately cooked which is compulsory to taste. Fresh fire is produced by way of extracting of dried wood with a piece of bamboo at jumping ground in the morning. After cooking, shouting of hoi will be performed for lunch and followed by the Gaan Ngai grand feast. Towards evening, long jump and shot put activities are carried out. Then Shaopaak Thetmei meaning greeting as well as warning is executed by elderly people. Boys and girls will spend dining together, indulged in merry making, drinking, eating, cutting jokes and perform a programme of Pazeimei in the village.

(ii) The 2nd Day – Tamchan Ngai

All the members of both boys' and girls' dormitories will bring their Tamcha meaning gift/subscription in the form of meat, vegetables, money etc. to their respective dormitories. The deceased family also brings last presentation called Thei-Tamcha in honour to the deceased who died in the previous year. A Banja who officiates as a priest will perform chanting the Tamsuan and Zousuan hymns for two seniormost Gaanpis and two heads of girls' dormitory. In the evening, Tamchan Laam, a ritual dance is performed by girls only (i) to the house of Pei, (ii) to the house of old women and (iii) to the house of Ganchang. Thus the second day of festival comes to an end.

(iii) The 3rd Day – Tuna Gaan Ngai

The 3rd day of festival is called Tuna Gaan Ngai, the festival of the youth. In the morning two Khangbon (heads of boys' dormitory) and two Tunapi (heads of girls' dormitory) will bring Tamcha to their respective dormitories. A Banja will recite the hymns of Tamsuan and Zousuan. After lunch, boys (holding a firewood each in their hands) will visit to the houses of the above four persons shouting hoi (Rilai hoi) and appreciate them for giving abundant gifts and wine. The boys pray to Tingkao Ragwang for longevity of life and giving strength to them.

In the evening, boys and girls will perform Khangbon Kadimei Laam (bidding farewell dance to Khangbon) if they are to be promoted to the post of Ganchang in that year. If no dance is to be performed for Khangbon, then a Laamleng (rotation) will be performed.

(iv) The 4th Day – Longkumei

Longkumei meaning hill trekking is performed on the fourth day. Boys and girls climb a nearby hill for sight seeing. Where there is no hill nearby, Longkumei is nominally performed at the northern village gate where some boys who are expert in the art of traditional drum beating use to beat the same. After that Gakting Tam (pork chutney), wine, boiled vegetables are offered to all present there. A Longkumei dance is performed at the village northern gate. Then Phakgang Laam (dance) is performed at the house of two boys and two girls.

(v) The 5th Day – Napchanmei

In the evening, a ritual ceremony of calling of paddy with a big cock to the boys and girls dormitories by a priest will be performed invoking the goddess of food grain to restore the wasted or missing rice. The cooked liver of the fowl, rice and crushed ginger will be offered to the goddess of Kambuipui, Charaipui and Kairao (ancestors) who live in the form of hearth stones in the house as per belief.

Napsin Gansin Raomei

It means criticism made to the leaders of male dormitory particularly against the Khangbons and immediate two seniormost Gaanpis for not being fed delicious dishes during the festival. This criticism is carried out through songs and not speech. This song is called Napchan Luh.

Singing competition at girls' dormitory

After that the members of boys' dormitory will proceed to the girls' dormitory for singing competition. On reaching there, an elder will offer holy wine to Tingkao Ragwang not to cause any disturbances during the course of singing competition. Then, boy will first sing the folk songs of romance etc. and followed by girl. If the singing competition is over, the members of boys' dormitory will return to boys' dormitory shouting rilai hoi. If willing, boys may perform a programme of going around the village singing the village guarding songs (Kailong Lonmei).

(vi) The 6th Day – Rangpatmei

Rangpatmei means worship to all gods of Zeliangrong pantheons. It I carried out on the last day of the festival. This ritual is performed at the abode of northern village deity. Its objective is to ward off any diseases, hardship, illness, death etc. The evil spirits are not worshipped but they are propitiated not to give trouble to men. This ritual is known as Raren Loumei. Violation of this restriction may happen even death etc. This is the reason behind the village gate is closed and man is not allowed to pass through the village gate while this ritual goes on. Another significance of closure of village gate is to stop the entry of evil spirits in the village. Every household will bring fowl, a piece of ginger and a bundle of banana leaf to the house of Pei for this ritual.

Raangpat Tamcha

One Banja announces to bring Raangpat Tamcha. Accordingly, Banja will bring Raangpat Tamcha such as eatables, local salt cakes which are distributed to all the Banjas. Gaanchang is not entitled to enjoy it.

Rangpat Puan

Male and girls' dormitories will give puan (in form of money) as a scapegoat (pumlin) of boys and girls to the members of Pei.

Khupot Laitatmei (collection and throw out pipe)

The hanging of pipe which was earlier distributed to every household to store epidemic diseases inside the pipe will be collected after pouring wine into the pipe and cover the mouth of the bamboo pipe with cotton and throw out beyond the village gate.

Maru Zou

A Banja informs the local people to come and collect the Maru Zou (blessed wine). It is good for health as believed by the followers of TRC.

Filling up the vacant posts

If there is any vacant post of Khunbu or Khunlak or other post before the Gaan Ngai festival, the vacant post is filled up by a seniormosr suitable person(s) by declaring with an iron-hoe by a Banja at the northern village gate in the name of Tingkao Ragwang.

Bukaomei

After this, old men and others will proceed with a rilai hoi to Peikai where a priest will conduct a ritual of Bukaomei (calling of souls) with a big cock. The cooked chicken pieces will be distributed to every household of the village for good health. Every member of the house should at least taste the piece of chicken for good health.

(vii) The 7th Day – Pontang Nimmei

Early in the morning, members of the village Pei and members of boys dormitory will gather at male dormitory and one of the Khangbons put some reasonable amount on paantangly (winnowing fan) requesting the village authority to accept the request amount. If accepted by the village authority will hand over the money to the wife of the patriach. The reason for giving money is for disturbing their sleep, breaking earthen pots containing wine (zoulai), lossof utensils etc. Thereafter Banja will offer holy wine to Tingkao Ragwang accompanied by distribution of chutney of dry eel or beef or pork and drink etc. to each and every member present. The same procedure will also be done at girls' dormitory. In the evening, young boys are taught by the Gaanpis by issuing whip (Thing-ngun kadimei) to improve the shortcoming faced during the festival. Thus, the Gaan Ngai festival comes to an end.

10. What is the duration of the festival in your village?

The Gaan Ngai festival lasts for seven days

11. Are all the traditional festivals performed in your village/community popular among the elders, youth (boys and girls) and women folk?

All the traditional festivals of Zeliangrong are popular to all kinds of sexes of different grades however youth are the most enthusiastic in the Gaan Ngai festival.

12. In what way the festival is concerned with women folk in the village with the festival? Describe their role or activities at home or village or dormitories during the festival.

Women folk participate in this festival if there is any promotion from women to old women in a particular year. Then individual family will arrange a community feast and followed by a promotional dance towards evening in honour to the promotee(s). If there is no promotion, involvement by womenfolk in this festival does not arise. If individual family makes a request for farewell dance, they will present the same in honour to the dead who died in previous year. This dance is not compulsory. Womenfolk have no role at village or dormitories in this festival. There is no feast in their dormitory. Special dance is supposed to be performed for the newly married women as an admission to their institution (Thien), the house of married women but this dance is now performed at the Rih-Ngai festival.

13. Do other communities participate in this festival?

No other communities in a group participate in this festival however individual friends are invited to the festival dinner. Some women and girls participate in the performance of dance as individual capacity.

14. Do you think that the festival should be popularized by the community and the state?

Yes, this festival should be opularised by the community at the same time, the participation of the State Govt. is also necessary for more popularity of this festival. Educated people should write article on Gaan Ngai festival to publish in the local newspapers etc.

(a) Mention some of the instances in which the Government extends financial assistance for this festival.

The Directorate for Development of Tribals and Scheduled Caste Manipur for rich observation of Gaan Ngai festival was pleased to accord sanction a sum of Rs. 5 lakhs in favour of the State Level Gaan Ngai Celebration Committee, Manipur for the year 20122 vide order No. 26/38/2004-TD (Mise) dated 11-01-2011. This issued with the concurrence of Finance Deptt. Vide UO No. 4/1010-2011/FD(14-p/23) Plan dated 11-01-2011.

15. What are the categories of dances performed during the festival?

There are three categories of dances performed during this festival. They are

(i) Tamchan Laam (Ritual dance)

(ii) Festival Dance:

(a) Longkumei Laam/Phaakgang Laam

(b) Khangbon Kadimei Laam

(c) Laamleng Laam

(d) Thei Kadimei Laam

(iii) Birds/Animals/Insects imitating dance

16. What is the nature of the songs performed during the festival? Give a description of the theme of the songs

The following songs are sung during the festival. They are (i) Laam luh, (ii) Napsin Gansin Raomei Luh (Napchan Luh), (iii) Kaihut Luh, (iv) Khamlen Luh, (v) Thensonmei Luh, (vi) Maja Luh, (vii) Ramron Luh, (viii) Kailong Lonluh, (ix) Luh Phai, (x) Thei Kadimei Luh etc.

(i) Laam Luh – means dancing song. A cultural dance is always associated with this song

(ii) Napsin Gansin Raomei Luh – this song is sung on the occasion of Napchanmei. The song itself criticizes the heads of boys' dormitory for not being served delicious dishes during the festival. The criticism is translated through songs.

(iii) Kaihut Luh – means praising the matriarch of the boys' and girls' dormitories. This song is also sung after the conclusion of the above song.

(iv) Khamlen luh – means opening song of door. This song is sung when boys come to girls' dormitory for singing competition there. The girls remain inside the girls' dormitory closing the door when this song is sung. The girls will also sing the same with the spirit of competition with the boys. As soon as the song ends, the girls will open the door. Then singing competition starts.

(v) Thensonmei Luh – meaning send off song of traditional institutions of boys' and girls' dormitories. This song is sung as conclusion after the completion of formal dance.

(vi) Maja Luh – means song of calling of paddy for good yield. This song is also sung at the singing competition. When the village guarding songs end and this song will be sung inside the individual house.

(vii) Ramron Luh – This is mourning or lamenting song sung mainly on the occasion of singing competition at girls' dormitory, farewell dance or parting feast occasion etc.

(viii) Kailong Lonluh – it is a village guarding song. The boys use to sing this song holding a spear each in their hands and going around the village at night to check any miscreants or enemies attack and to guard the village from looting and theft. When boys go around the village singing this song, the villagers are warm in their mind and free from any kind of tension.

(ix) Theikadimei Luh – this song is sung on the occasion of farewell dance presented in honour to the dead who died in the previous year.

(x) Luh Phai – It is a romatic song. Boys sing this song conveying his love to his girl friend whom he loves.

17. What are the religious rites performed during the festival?

The rites are as follows –

(i) Gucheng Phaimei – It is a ritual performed by an elder early in the morning of the first day of the festival at the abode of the village deity called Kaipi Bambu and Kaiba Bambu not to happen any untowards incident during the festival.

(ii) Calling of Paddy – It is performed at boys' and girls' dormitories on the day of Napchanmei by a priest. Its objective is to restore the missing or wasted rice during the festival.

(iii) Raren Loumei – It is the worship of all kinds of gods believed by the Zeliangrong people performed at the northern gate of the village on the concluding day of the festival. The main objective of this ritual is for prosperity and well being and not to cuase any kind of trouble, sickness, death etc. in the village.

(a) Mention the community and individual rituals performed during the festival.

The community rituals are performed during the festival as stated above and individual ritual of calling of paddy is also performed on the first day of the festival towards evening by a priest.

18. What measures should be taken up by the community and social leaders to preserve this festival? Give your recommendations.

The Zeliangrong people are observing this festival regularly and annually. However for better observance of this festival, a programme of seminar, symposium, discussion on question and answer, lecture should be organized before the commencement of this festival every year. Teaching and learning of cultural dances are to be performed. The boys should also learn and practice the traditional drum beating producing different sounds (Khongluan) which are quite essential to use on the occasion of Taraang Kai Shumei, Maku Banru, Bamjou Jangmei, Ragaidai etc. All people irrespective of age should digest the philosophy or concept of the festival. From Khangbon to every member of boys' and girls' dormitories should learn all kinds of songs sung in the festival. All the members of Pei should also learn the ritual activities, hymns etc. Without the above elements, the celebration of Gaan Ngai festival is meaningless.

Lanbilung Gonmei's response covering the festivals of Zeme, Liangmei and Puimei are reproduced. The respondent is an M.A. in History, a Selection Grade Lecturer of History of Imphal College and a religious leader. Some portions of his response to the questionnaire are reproduced.

"2. Name of the community

Rongmei of Zeliangrong group

(a) What are the cognate groups of the Zeliangrong?

The cognate groups of the Zeliangrong are Zeme, Liangmai, Rongmei and Puimei

(b) Is the respondent aware of the Zeliangrong solidarity movement?

Yes, the respondent is aware of the Zeliangrong solidarity movement.

(c) If yes, give a brief account

The kindred groups Zeme, Liangmai, Rongmei and Puimei have common ethno-cultural origin. In the due course of migration and history of past have come to inherit the present names.

The movement of solidarity was feasibly begun with Haipou Jadonang and Rani Gaidinliu (1905-1993). The solidarity movement was crystallized only in 1947. On 15th February of the year at Keishamthong, the Zeliangrong Naga Council was formed with the objective of strong and closer affinity of the cognate groups of the same origin. Later on, Zeliangrong Peoples' Convention was emerged with the political tune and more organizations, women society, students' union were established to foster the feeling of solidarity. The Zeliangrong Peoples' Convention established in 1980 at Tamenglong and went more than the racial unity and solidarity. The Zeliangrong Peoples' Convention had adopted administrative ideology. At present solidarity movement and divergence movement are working in the opposite.

3. What are the religious beliefs of the Zeliangrong Community?

The religious belief of the Zeliangrong community is known as primordial religion in which culture is the integral part of religion. The religion has been in the continuation since the immoral times. The belief of the cognate groups is centred around the Creator God – Tingkao Ragwang. When Zeme and Liangmai know him Tingwang, the Rongmei address him Tingkao Ragwang.

From the creator God – Tingkao Ragwang, different tributaries of religions cults have been evolved. From the common parent Goddistinct religion philosophies are developed. The different cults of traditional religion are Heraka, Tingkao Ragwang Chapriak, Pou-pei Chap and Champa.

4. Give an account of the Zeliangrong Heraka religion. Who was the founder of Heraka and who were the followers of this cult?

The Heraka religion of the Zeliangrong is primordial in the conceptual assessment. The world and the universe begun with Tingkao Ragwang. His son Banglagwang first came and ruled over the earth. The rule of Banglagwang may be identified with Sudimpu of TRC. The wife of Banglagwang was Jigale and daughter was Kamadinlu. The rule of Banglagwang over the earthly affairs was assisted by a priest named Herakandingpau. The name of Heraka was derived from Herakandingpau.

Haipou Jadonang was the pioneer in the evolution of Heraka religion. He gave due emphasis of worship to Tingkao Ragwang. Rani Gaidinliu formalized the coming of Heraka religion. Zeme, Liangmai and Rongmei are the followers of Heraka religion.

5. What is the Tingkao Ragwang Chapriak (TRC) of the Zeliangrong people? Give a brief account of this religious system.

Tingkao Ragwang Chapriak of the Zeliangrong people is the traditional and indigenous religion. It is primordial in concept and theory.

Tingkao Ragwang Chapriak is unique among the different cults of the Zeliangrong belief. Among the traditional gods and goddesses, emphasis is given to Tingkao Ragwang. He constilitates all the gods and goddesses like magnate around him. Other earthly gods and goddesses represent His will. Tingkao Ragwang Chapriak bears the following tenets in short (i) it emphasizes the worship of Tingkao Ragwang, (ii) it advocates devotion and simplicity over ritual and sacrifices, (iii) ritual and sacrifices are still continuing as the inherit parts of the belief, (iv) it worships other gods and goddesses of the lower realm, (v) festivals are the integral parts of worship in the religion and culture both cognitive and behavioural dimensions are the vehicle of the religious system.

6. Please mention the names of the festivals performed by the cognate groups of the Zelaingrong people with (a) Month and season, (b) Significance and (c) a brief description.

I. The festivals of the Rongmeis (are omitted)

II. Festivals of Zeme

a) Hega Ngi: It is the festival of purification of mind and body of men to have the success of life in the year to come. It is celebrated for about five to six days in the month of January. On the commencing day of the festival, the members of Rehangki do not eat the meal prepared by women. The procession of ho-hoimg is followed by long jump and stone throwing. The members of Rehangki and Releki climb peak to hunt animal and fish. Competitions of folk songs are held between unmarried members of Rehangki and Releki. Only women dances are performed during the festival.

b) Herasam Ngi: It is a seed sowing festival. It is held for four days. In the festival four footed animal is sacrificed by two men having tied to the wooden post. The meal of the sacrificed animal shall be eaten only by the Zeme. Each dormitory shall sacrifice cock and the pieces of chicken are distributed to all the families.

   The horns, bones and hairs of the sacrificed four footed animal is kept in secret. This festival is celebrated in the month of May. The significance of this festival is the prayer to grow the plants healthy from seeds.

c) Loitue Ngi: It is the festival of youths. In this festival the old people of neighbours and clan arrange meal and drink and feed the youths of their neighbours. In the early days it was held at the dormitories. This festival is celebrated in the month of August. The significance of this festival is to promote the health and body of the youths.

d) Langsim ngi: It is the festival of old aged people. The youthd of neighbours and clans joined together and arrange meal and drink for the old aged people of the segment of the locality. The festival is celebrated in the month of September for one day. The significane of this festival is respect and regard of the old aged people. They are considered to the structure of the society.

e) Hekak Ngi: It is the festival of the departed soul who passed away in the previous year. It is held for two days. In the festival, the bereaved family offer food to the departed soul on the grave by killing animal. Some flesh of the sacrificed animal is distributed to neighbours and families of the village. The bereaved family mourns for the departed soul. This festival held is held in the month of December. The significance of this festival is the prayer and mourning for the departed soul and the departed soul are becoming divine being and totem of the family. Source: Hejating, Jangkholen, Senapati district, 6-1-2012.

III. Festivals of the Liangmai

The following are the festivals of Liangmai with months, significance and also the things done during the festival.

a) Chaga Ngi: It is the biggest festival of Liangmai. It is held for three days. The important activities are Chong-phenmei, dance, folk songs. These activities are carried by the Luchuki, Khangchuki and Peiki. It is held during the last part of October. The significance of this festival is the festival of prayer to avoid the hurdles and difficulties of life and it is the evolution from the early character of warrior of festival.

b) Mutui Ngi: It is the festival of sesamum because sesamum become the main item of consumption in the festival. It is observed for one day. In the festival grinded sesamum is added to the curries in every household. The mixing of sesamum to the curries is compulsory. It is celebrated in the month of Novemeber. The significance of this festival is the indication that sesamum preparation with other items of food is required in ritual and ceremonies and it is an indigenous crop.

c) Gen Ngi: It is the festival of the departed soul who passed away after the preceding Gen Ngi. This festival is held for two days. During the festival, the bereaved individual families have collected stones and these stones are laid on the graves. Food and meals are offered to the departed souls. It is held in the month of Gen Hu of the local lunar calendar. Sports such as long jump, wrestling and stone throwing are held but no shon is given. It is probably held in the month of September.

d) Tashot Manah Ngi: It is a seed sowing festival. It is held for two days. During the festival two unmarried men are selected by Peiki. The two go to the village Rang (gate) to collect the seeds. The seeds are placed in the proper place near the village gate which cannot be easily harmed by animals, insects and pests. The two unmarried men covered their heads by shawl came to collect the seeds and were accompanied by other members with ho-hoing. They finally marched to Peiki. From Peiki, seeds are distributed to the families of the village. On these days, the village is closed to the others. It is known as genna which is a sort of prayer and worship. It is observed in the local lunar month of Kare Hu, in the month of February. The significance of this festival is the prayer and worship to God that divine blessing is required for healthy growth of crops and plants.

e) Kabui Dui Ngi: It is a festival celebrated for married daughters of the village. This festival is held for three days. The duration of the festival is fixed collectively by peiki. The married daughters are fed by the parents. It is held in May. The significance of this festival is love and respect to the married daughters by parents.

f) Duilong Ngi: It is the blessing festival. It is held for two days. On the commencing day of the festival, the two elders of Peiki shall proceed on the public path to give blessing to the members of Khangchukis from one point to another point. The Khangchukis 9male dormitories) are ready to receive the elders. When the two elders approach to the Khangchukis, they draw different lines on the floor indicating animal, crops and others and given blessing by proclamation. It is held in Kapi-Hu of local lunar calendar and it is in the month of June. The festival inspires the youths to work hard in hunting and cultivation.

g) Maraup Ngi: It is the festival of prediction of dream and hope. It is held for one day. In the festival shooting arrows from bow are held by the members of Khangchuki. The achievement of targets is considered that hope and dreams shall be ensured. The shooting are held with the religions ritual and prayer. It is held in the month of July. The significance of this festival is the prayer and worship for hope and dream.

h) Mishuan ngi: It is the festival of daughters both married and unmarried. It is held for one day. Married daughters outside the villages are invited. They are fed by parents and brothers. The festival is held in the month of August which is also known as Kham-Hu in local lunar calendar.

Source: Kailamdin Chawang, Tharon, Tamenglong district, Manipur, 22-12-2011

IV. Festivals of the Puimei

The following are the festivals of the Puimei

a) Chaga Mangei: this festival is also known Manggeipui Mangei because of addition to the Chaga Mangei in the recent past. It is held for about five days. At present, the beginning of the festival is fixed on 13th Wakching, the Manipuri lunar calendar and it is in the month of January. On the first day morning Gokpai Jaomei – observation of the spleen of pig is held which is attended by male members. in the afternoon all the members of Katang inn proceed to the northern gate- Lhang and return to the south of the village gate with ho-hoing and finally stop at the place of sport where long jump, stone throwing are held. After the sport, new fire is extracted and is distributed to all the families of the village. The members of Katang inn ultimately proceed to their Katang inn (bachelor dormitory). The night meal is prepared from the sacrificed pig and only boys take the meal. It is meant only for the members of Katang inn. Men and women are separated and it is called Pumthanmei – purification of body and mind. On the seond day of the festival, two banana plants are brought at Katang inn and they are erected at the northern and southern gates of the village. A ceremony known as Chong-Phenmei is held beginning at the north and then to the south. The Chong-Phenmei ritual which is translated as prediction of victory for four hopes and dreams – to marry a girl of his choice, to harvest crops as large as he dreams, to hunt the number of animal as he target and to win over the enemies. It is the shooting of arrows on the banana plant. After the conclusion at northern and southern gates, the members of Katang inn gather at the place of sport where they perform the ritual jam-mei. It is the pronouncement of hymn by the elders with spears that they shall be blessed to overcome the enemies. Then the boys go to their dormitories of priest or elders. A cock is sacrificed to bestow upon them blessing and it is performed by elder known Likaomei. The sacrificed cock is cooked with salt, ginger and chilly only. In evening all the boys and girls of Katang inn and Langnga inn take meals to each house. It is known as the beginning of new meal. On the third day of the festival, one boy and one girl are selected for best preparation of drink and curry. In honour of their specialization in preparing drink and curry, dance are performed to them. The category of drink is done for girl and the other is meant for bot. married women also perform dancein the next day of the festival. The festival has the significance of reviving the social and religious belief of the Puimeis.

b) Nabit Mangei: It is the festival of the newly born infants. This festival is held for teo or three days. In the festival, a ceremony known as Chapon Mu is held for the newly born infants. The families who have new born babies have to offer sweets and etables to the old people at their dormitory. At the conclusion of the festival, propitiation to gods and goddesses are held to purify the village. The festival is held in the month of March or Lamta of the Manipuri lunar calendar. The festival has the significance of love and respect to the newly born infants and old aged people.

c) Kathing Dui Inno Mangei: It is the seed sowing festival. It is held for one day in the month of May which is Kalen according to Manipuri lunar calendar. Each family perform ritual with a cock at the main door of their respective houses. This ritual is the prayer for prosperity and good harvest. A sport of tug of war is held. The significance of this festival is the consideration of the requirement of divine blessing for good harvest.

d) Pokpha Mangei: It is the festival celebrated to offer the newly harvested grain to the creator God. A cock is sacrificed in ritual by each family of the village to harvest more crops and grains. This festival is held in the month of July. The significance of this festival is the acknowledgement of the divine hand in harvesting.

e) Tatak Muidangu Mangei: It is the festival held for the departed soul. It is held for two days. The person who had passed away after harvesting, is considered to be the first death of the commencing year. Ceremony is held by bereaved family and joined by the villagers. Wooden posts are erected around grave and hanging bars are made available from the posts. Eatables are hung at the hanging bars over the grave. Homage and tributes are paid to the departed souls. Folk songs are sung overnight. This festival is held in the month of Decmber which is the Poinu month of Manipuri lunar calendar.

Source: Abuiba Gonmei, Changangei village, Imphal West District, 14-1-2012.

(Note: This questionnaire given by respondent Lanbilung Gonmei, research consultant deals with the festivals of the Zeme, Liangmai and the Puimei cognate groups.)

ANNEXURE II

Festival Songs Adopted in Majorkhul During the Gaan Ngai Festival

Some selected ones are given below both in Rongmei and English version

Rongmei	English version

1. Phaiseng laam Iu: The dancers approaching to the house of the honoured one

Goipong Takon changhu-lana	With elephants and horses leading us in the front
Kumeipui-ta andong nahom gangpuboi	We have come to honour you (name of the honoured one)
Anthem-mei kin pat jao-lo	Please come out and see our dormitory dancers
Dandi kachak ampon puna gangpuboi	Have come dressed in silver and gold
Anthem-mei kin patjao nimei	People who wish to witness us (out dormitory)
Kailong lakhou dingpang nikum bambuwe	Are gathered in the courtyard in full
Sing-Lama Kumei-pu jao to hounina	They wish to have a glimpse of you, honoured one.
Raangdai anlong anjon kumna gangpuboi	Like the flight of the hornbill, they come to see you.

2. Phaiseng–laam lu: Praising the honoured one

Hei Namthan khou mei-lung meigoi	Oh! All the residents of our village, Namthanlong
Achampei-ta aloinimei naichou?	Is there anyone who can compete with goddess of animal (Champei)?

Aram Namthan khouni	In our village, Namthanlong
Kumei puta racham dinkum bambuwei	You are the famed one
Hey, khani tungam-mak	Hey, Your meat and fish are inexhaustible.
Jou-ni jangam maklonne	Your beer cannot be completely consumed

3. Phaiseng-laam lu: Praising the honoured one

Kumei-pukai kaima nung	In the beautiful courtyard of the honoured one
Arambang daimei thaokham namin	A banyan tree is growing with its ripe fruits
Bambuwe	
Kakun khat-tho Rangdai sao	The hornbill sitting in a branch
Kakun khat-tho Loingao saobam-buwe	The shrike (Loingao) is chirping
Chidun gainung Rangdai samgang	The hornbill is sitting on a best branch
Gangtou-na sao bambuwe	And singing

Pajei-Lu

Rongmei	*English version*
1. Ringa-khang rangthao then-kan meigoi	O' the girls who were married before the Gaan Ngai
Akin-ta houlana	Seeing us, the boys and girls of the village
Kakai-thu gangdatla su,	Sitting at home unhappy
Then keila kamik ang-gan ta phang bambuwe,	Retiring from her dormitory, looking at the boys.

Then kei-likho	O' Themlainei, let us not get
Themlainei-le anei kin	married
Athei chabon kinsong	Than the days of the yore
Atao chabon kin-gai ringa tallakge	Today's better and let us enjoy
2. Hei Chonglainei, hei-lao kumkan etuwe,	O' Chonglainei has gone to the paddy field
Neikhem keitei gangda jaiyo	Return home early before the sunset.
Nang-bam mangna kailong anchu etuwe	Without you, the village looks forlorn
Chonglainei jao hou-mangna	Chonglainei, the day you are not seen
Neirin bamjing thui-mangei	I cannot bear staying alone. (Chonglainei is a popular title given to a girl by the youths)
3. Hey! ansei-the, ansei deithe lamlu tamu	Hey! Today is the day, today is the day of my love
Ansei deithe anei bamna ringa na bamkhang,	Today is the day we sit together and enjoy our company.
Nangni kaipi meipui su.	When married, you will be a housewife of the northern side of the village
Aini kaiba ang-gan sukhang deithe,	I will be a youth of the lower side of the village
Ansei deithe anei bamna ringa na bamkhang,	Today is the day of our rejoicing.

Bibliography

A.K. Abbott, Notes on the Naga Hills and the Narrative of a Military Expedition into Kacha Naga Country during Feb-April, 1881 reproduced in Elwin, Nagas in the Nineteenth Century, Bombay, 1969

Achenbou Nuimai, Chagaa Gadi festival and its significance, *Nagaland Post*, Dimapur, 30-10-2010

All Zeliangrong Students' Union (Assam, Manipur and Nagaland), *A Brief Account of Zeliangrong Nagas*, Dimapur, 2009

Asoso Yunou, *The Naga Struggle against the British under Jadonang and Rani Gaidinliu,* Kohima, 1984

C.A. Soppit, A Short Account of the Kachcha Naga (Empeo) *Tribe in North Cachar Hills with an outline Grammar, Vocabulary and Illustrative Sentences*, Shillong, 1885

Chaoba Kamson (ed), *Gaan-Ngai A Festival of Zeliangrong People*, Imphal, 2003

Chaoba Kamson (ed), *Ringlon-Theilon*, published by Zeliangrong Religious Council, Imphal, 2002

Chaoba Kamson (ed), *Socio-cultural and Spiritual Traditions of Zeliangrongs*, Guwahati, 2011

Chaoba Kamson (ed), *Sovenir 116 years of Thendai Khangchu*, Imphal, 2008

Chaoba Kamson, *Philosophy of Gaan-Ngai*, Imphal, 2010

Chaoba Kamson, *The Philosophical concept of Tingkao Ragwang Chapriak*, Imphal, 2011

E.W. Dun, *The Gazetteer of Manipur*, Simla, 1886

Ethel St. Claire Grimwood, *My Three Years in Manipur*, London, 1891

Fifty Years of Zeliangrong Movement, 1927-1977, Golden Jubilee Committee, Tening, 1977

G. Makuga, *An Introduction to Rongmei Nagas*, Imphal, 1993

G. Makuga, *The Rongmei Customary Laws,* Dimapur, 2007

Gangmumei Kamei, *A History of the Zeliangrong Nagas From Makhel to Rani Gaidinliu*, Guwahati, 2004

Gangmumei Kamei, *Essays on Primordial Religion,* New Delhi, 2005

Gangmumei Kamei, *Jadonang A Mystic Naga Rebel,* 3rd edn., Imphal, 2009

Gangmumei Kamei, *Tingkao Ragwang Chapriak: The Zeliangrong Primordial Religion*, Imphal, 2005

George A. Grierson, *Linguistic Survey of India,* Vol. 3: Tibeto-Burman family Part II, Calcutta, 1908

Heraka: *The Primordial Religion and its Revitalization Movement*, published by Zeliangrong Heraka Association, North East India, Haflong, 2011

Herakame Leu published by Zeliangrong Heraka Association, Haflong, 2009

Hurui Zeliang, Rani *Gaidinliu - The Mother of us all*, Dimapur, 21-01-2010

J. Roy, *A History of Manipur*, Calcutta, 1958: 1973

Jadonang, *A Freedom Fighter of Manipur, a commemorative volume*, 1970, Imphal

James Johnstone, *My Experience in Manipur and Naga Hills*, London, 1896

Jawaharlal Nehru, *A bunch of old letters,* Bombay, 1960 (Some letters on Rani Gaidinliu and Jadonang)

Julian Jacob, *The Nagas, The Hill People of North East India*, London, 1990

K.S. Singh, *Tribal Movements in India,* Vol.1, Delhi, 1982

Kaikhamang Daimei, *Chagah Festivals and its significance,* Imphal, unpublished paper

L.W. Shakespeare, *A History of the Assam Rifles,* London, 1929, reprint Gauhati/Delhi, 1981

Majorkhul Khangchu, published by S. Khangmeidun and Ph. Gaikompu, Imphal, 2011

M.P. Namthiurei, *The Great Awakening*, Tamenglong, 1972

N.B. Pamei, *The Trail from Makuilongdi,* Shillong

N.C. Zeliang, *Herakame Leu,* Kohima, 1974

N.C. Zeliang, *Zeliangrong Heraka Movement and socio-cultural awakening in Naga society*, Dimapur, 2005

Pautanzan Newme, *Zeliangrong Customary Laws*, Published by Zeliangrong Heraka Association, Assam, Manipur and Nagaland, Haflong, 2009

Prakash Singh, *Nagaland*, National Book trust, Delhi, 1972

R. Constantine, *Manipur, Maid of the Mountains*, Delhi, 1980

R. Marulung, *Naga Dharma*, Imphal, 1988

R. Marulung, *Rongmei Naga Phunga Wari,* Imphal, 1984

R. Marulung, *Zeliangrong Wari Singbun*, Imphal, 1996

R. Steward, *Notes on Northern Cachar Hills,* Calcutta, 1955

R.B. Pemberton, *A Report on the Eastern Frontier of British India* 1835, Reprint 1966, Gauhati (relevant portion)

R.B. Pemberton, *The Nagas in Wilson's Documents of the Burmese War, Calcutta,* 1827 reproduced in Verrier Elwin's Nagas in the nineteenth century, Oxford University Press, 1969

R.K. Ringthim, *Odyssey A Brief account of the Zeliangrong Struggle for Freedom and Peace,* Shillong, 2009

Ragongning Gangmei, *Common Folk Songs of the Rongmei*, Imphal, 1994

Ramkhun Pamei, *The Zeliangrongs,* New Delhi, 1996

Ramkuiwangbe Newme, *Tingwang Hinde (in Zeme),* Haflong, 1991

Robert Brown, *A Statistical Account of Manipur,* Calcutta, 1974

Robert Reid, *A History of Frontier Areas bordering Assam 1884-1941,* Shillong, 1942, reprint, 1997, Guwahati

S.K. Chatterjee, *Kirata Jana Kriti,* JASB, Calcutta, 1952, 1970

S.P. Sen (Ed), *Dictionary of National Biography*, Institute of Historical Studies, Calcutta, 1972. Biographical notes on Jadonang and Rani Gaidinliu

S.P. Tungchapbo, Post-modern understanding of Chaga Gadi for social transformation, *Nagaland Post*, 1 November, 2011 (Chaga Gadi or Chaga Ngi is the greatest festival of the Liangmai of the Zeliangrong community)

Stephen Fuchs, *The Rebellious Prophets,* Bombay, 1965

Sujata Miri, *Liangmai Naga Stories and Legends*, Delhi, 1982

T.C. Hodson, *The Naga Tribes of Manipur,* London, 1911

Tasile N. Zeliang, *Ranipuri Gaidinliu Pajat Tin Thiu Khaibo* (Biography of Rani Gaidinliu in Liangmai) with a foreword by Professor Gangmumei Kamei, Guwahati, 2008

Tunchapbo, S.P, Chaga Gadi, *Nagaland Post,* Dimapur, 30-10-2010

U.G. Bower, *Naga Path*, John Murray, London, 1950, reprint Guwahati/Delhi, 2003

Vierrer Elwin, *Nagas in Nineteenth Century*, Bombay, 1969. This book contains 15 articles on the Zeliangrong Nagas

William McCulloch, *An Account of the Valley of Munnipore and the surrounding Hill Tribes with a comparative vocabulary of Munnipore and other languages,* Calcutta, 1859

Zeliangrong Religious Council, *Luh khatni Kasoi, Tingkao Ragwang Chapriak,* edited time to time. The latest publication was 2012

Glossary

Banza	The highest age grade elder of a Rongmei village
Chakak Ngi (Ngai)	Ceremony of the parting of the spirits of the dead from the village equivalent Hekak Ngi (Zeme), Chakak Ngi (Liangmai) and Chakak Ngai (Rongmei)
Chaga Ngi	Festival of the Liangmai; Chaga Gadi is a new term used by them
Dan jaomei	Taking the omen by ginger on the first day of Gaan Ngai
Gaan Ngai	Festival of the winter season
Gakpai-jaomei	Interpreting the spleen of the pig to see the omen
Ganchang	Middle age grade elder of the Rongmeis
Genna	A Naga worshipping day, from the Angami word Kenna
Heraka	Literal meaning in Zeme "not impure" (pure); name of a reformed religion of the Zeliangrong people started by Rani Gaidinliu
Hoi gammei	The procession of the male populace of a Zeliangrong village by ho-hoing through the village

Kadepeo	Head of the village, of Zeme origin
Khangbon	Leaders of the male dormitory of the Rongmeis
Khullakpa	Administrator of the village; of Meitei origin
Khunpu	Owner of the village (Nampou) of Meitei origin
Morung	Dormitory of a Naga village, the word is of unknown origin, equivalent to Dekachang of the Assamese, Pakhangphan of the Meiteis and Zualbuk of the Mizos
Mithun	Bos frontalis a domesticated variety of the Indian Bison
Napchanmei	The last day of Gaan Ngai; literal meaning offering of rice to the goddess presiding over the hearth of a house. The worship of goddess of Paddy known as Napkaomei is held on this occasion
Neihmei	Genna in Rongmei
Pei/Peikai	Office of the Village Council
Peipeo	Head of the village unit of Heraka
Tingkao Ragwang	Supreme God (God of the Sky) equivalent to Tingwang
TRC	Abbreviation of Tingkao Ragwang Chapriak, religion of Tingkao Ragwang
Zeliangrong	An acronym of the prefixes of the cognate groups of Zeme, Liangmai and Rongmei (Ze+Liang+Rong = Zeliangrong)

Index